Taking the Templar Habit:
Rule, Initiation Ritual, and the Accusations
against the Order
By Johnathan Edgeller

Acknowledgments

I am particularly grateful to the financial and emotional support from my friends, family, and God. My parents, Thomas and Jackie, and my sister Megan helped me during my graduate studies while I took my course work and while I was writing this thesis. I would especially like to thank my wife Kristin for being so understanding on my behalf for the lack of time I have been able to share with her in the final stages of this project. Her love and support has been essential to my continued progress.

I would also like to thank the people and students of the Texas Tech History Department for their resources and support during the research, and writing stages of this project. Special mention goes to Professors Stefano D'Amico, Barbara Hahn, and Patricia Pelley for their encouragement during my Masters studies. Special thanks go to Dave McDaniel for being an excellent graduate mentor.

I am especially indebted to my chair and advisor, Professor John Howe of Texas Tech University for his continued encouragement, support, and his invaluable expertise in working on this thesis. His help and guidance throughout my coursework and graduate career has been wonderful.

Table of Contents

Chapter I

Introduction

No other subject has ever inspired
more hacks from more countries throughout
time than the Templars.

–Umberto Eco[1]

Originally the Poor Knights of the Temple of Solomon were
fewer than a dozen knights, pilgrim knights who had sworn to protect
travellers to the Holy Land. Their seal exalted this humility by showing
two knights sharing one horse. However, as the west learned of these
strange but inspiring "warrior-monks," donations and recruits began to
come from far and wide. By 1170 about 300 knights in the Kingdom of
Jerusalem were responsible for defending many of the kingdom's
strategically important sites. From the Second Crusade onward, the
Templars were usually in the vanguard of crusader armies, maintaining
discipline and structure on the march for any leader's rank and file. Their
military prowess was demonstrated in actions throughout the
Mediterranean, including their bravery at the Battle of Montisgard in
1177 and their great sacrifices on the front line at Las Navas de Tolosa in
1212. The Templars built some of the largest and most high-tech castles
the west had ever known. By the 1250s, they were the church's largest

---

[1] Found in the forward to Barbara Frale, *The Templars: The Secret
History Revealed*, trans. Gregory Conti (New York: Arcade Publishing,
2009), xii.

1

military institution and the most influential standing army in Holy Land. They not only became the experts on fighting in the east, but also had set up an international banking system to finance and facilitate the crusade endeavors of Christendom's elite. Kings, such as Richard Lionheart and Louis IX, had access not only to the Templar's considerable coin but also to their troops, diplomatic and linguistics skills, and fortresses.

By the dawn of the fourteenth century, the elites of Christendom, and even the pope, were borrowing vast sums of money from the Templar coffers. King Philip IV of France was deeply in debt to the Templars due to his wars in Flanders and against Edward I of England. To pay, he began to tax the clergy in his domains. This led to the battle with Pope Boniface VIII over taxation rights which resulted in his demise in 1303. By 1305 Philip was able to negotiate with a French pope, Clement V, who held his court in France. With Philip's newfound authority over the taxation of clergy, other papal properties such as the Templars were now in his sight.

Unfortunately for the Templars, their meteoric rise was followed by an even more spectacular fall. Despite their bravest efforts at Acre in 1291, the Templars had lost all territory in Palestine within months. Grand Master of the Templars, James of Molay, had desperately attempted to regain a stronghold in the Holy Land by forging alliances with the Mongols. He even led a disastrous siege of the island of Ruad outside Tortosa which resulted in a huge defeat shortly after by the Egyptian Mamlukes. Each failure was a stain on their reputation as well as on that of the Church. James of Molay was called to France in 1307 to meet with Clement to discuss the matter of merging the Templars with their rivals, the Knights Hospitallers. While the grandmaster was in France, he spent some time meeting with Clement, with whom he had discussed rumors of heresy within the Templars. Although James denied all charges, Philip and Clement began to discuss the matter. Soon Philip took swift action.

On Friday, October 13th, 1307, Philip had all of the Templars throughout the domains of France arrested in one surprising blow. Lamenting "a thing terrible to contemplate, horrible to hear," Phillip charged the Templars with heresy, blasphemy, and homosexuality. After years of imprisonment and severe torture, many of the French Templars confessed to these crimes. Because their reputation was irrevocably damaged, Clement disbanded them and gave their property to their rivals, the Knights Hospitaller. On March 22, 1312, Clement's Papal bull, *Vox in excelso* suppressed the Templars definitively. He ordered that,

> Indeed, although legal process against the Order up to now does not permit its canonical condemnation as heretical by definitive sentence, the good name of the Order has been largely taken away by the heresies attributed to it. Moreover, an almost indefinite number of individual members, among whom are the grand master, the visitor of France and the chief preceptors, have been convicted of such heresies, errors and crimes through their spontaneous confessions. These confessions render the Order very suspect, and the infamy and suspicion render it detestable to the holy Church of God, to her prelates, to kings and other rulers, and to Catholics in general. It is also believed in all probability that from now on there will be found no good person who wishes to enter the Order, and so it will be made useless to the Church of God and the carrying on of the undertaking to the Holy Land, for which service the knights had been destined.[2]

---

[2] "Vox in excelso," in Malcolm Barber, and Keith Bate, *The Templars: Selected Sources Translated and Annotated* (New York: Manchester University Press, 2002), 309.

3

Clement had been losing ground in the fight against King Philip IV of France for years. Despite an attempt at absolving the Templars of their heresies at Chinon in August 1308, he ultimately decided that their reputation was too tarnished and that the Order had to be disbanded. By ending the controversy with Philip, and avoiding the fate of his predecessor Pope Boniface VIII, he not only saved himself but he also saved as much of the Templar properties as he could by handing them over to the Knights Hospitaller.[3]

In March of 1314, James of Molay renounced his previous confessions and proclaimed innocence for the Templars. Despite the destruction of the Templars in 1312, he had still been in Philip's clutches in a Parisian prison. He was immediately burned at the stake on the *Île de la Cité* facing Notre Dame. After his death, legends grew of the curse of James of Molay, the last Templar grand master who, as he burned, allegedly cursed both Clement and Philip. Within a year, both were dead: Philip in a hunting accident and Clement from illness.

The abrupt collapse of the once mighty Templars invites speculation. Not only were there popular legends, like James of Molay's curse, but some of the greatest contemporary minds of the time offered their views on the Templar fall. Almost immediately, Dante Alighieri mentions Philip IV, King of France, as the "modern Pilate" whose greed "to the temple bears his sordid sails" and Pope Clement V as "Christ's vicar" made "captive." His *Divine Comedy* claims that Philip had suppressed the Templars for monetary gain.[4] The theme of "the rise and

---

[3] Phillip deducted a considerable fee for his expenses.

[4] Dante, *The Divine Comedy,* trans. Henry Wadsworth Longfellow (New York: Barnes & Noble, 2008), 400.

fall of the Templars" is apparent in 15th-century Germany, when Dominican Felix Fabri wrote, "Albeit their beginning was holy and full of virtue, yet afterwards they degenerated from their forerunners after they waxed fat, and were spread about throughout the earth."[5]

Unfortunately, the Knights Templar left little written evidence of their identity. Their archives have been lost, and what remains is international detritus, largely the ruins of castles, priories, and churches. Except for a few letters, contracts, and papal bulls, the majority of Templar documents are trial records. This has made it difficult for historians to put together the fragments of data that remain into a grand narrative and has opened the door for charlatans and conspiracy theorists to invent a Templar identity far from reality. In the eighteenth century, Edward Gibbon's *The Decline and Fall of the Roman Empire* briefly attempted to define the Templar fall.

> But the firmest bulwark of Jerusalem was founded on the knights of the Hospital of St. John, and of the temple of Solomon; on the strange association of a monastic and military life, which fanaticism might suggest, but which policy must approve. The flower of the nobility of Europe aspired to wear the cross, and to profess the vows, of these respectable orders; their spirit and discipline were immortal; and the speedy donation of twenty-eight thousand farms, or manors, enabled them to support a regular force of cavalry and infantry for the defense of Palestine. The austerity of the convent soon evaporated in the exercise of arms; the world was scandalized by the pride, avarice, and corruption of these Christian soldiers; their claims of immunity and jurisdiction disturbed the harmony of the church and state; and the public peace was endangered by their jealous emulation. But in their most dissolute

---

[5] Malcolm Barber, *The New Knighthood: A History of the Order of the Temple* (Cambridge: Cambridge University Press, 1995), 315.

period, the knights of the Hospital and Temple maintained their fearless and fanatic character; they neglected to live, but they were prepared to die, in the service of Christ; and the spirit of chivalry, the parent and offspring of the crusades, has been transplanted by this institution from the holy sepulcher to the isle of Malta.[6]

Gibbon's contemporaries, not as reliant on the meager sources, used this gap in the historical narrative for their own gain. Freemasonry incorporated the Templars into its own creation myth, using them to give legitimacy and esoteric reality to their "history." Andrew Michael Ramsay, Chancellor of the Grand Lodge in France, crafted in 1737 a new origin story for the Scottish Rite of Freemasonry, which later incorporated the Templars as one of their forbearers.[7] This was the beginning of a long tradition associating the Templars with the likes of the Illuminati, the Freemasons, and the Priory of Sion as central suspects of all modern conspiracy theory.

The Templars gained more notoriety with 2003's *The Da Vinci Code* where Dan Brown was able to write a fictional novel based upon 1982's *The Holy Blood and the Holy Grail*. Despite the fact that the foundational "evidence" of both has been proven a hoax, Templar-mania has reached its modern day height. Although the blockbuster achievements of *The Da Vinci Code* may have driven popular perceptions towards scandal as Philip's propaganda had during the Templar trials, historians have attempted to continue in Gibbon's footsteps to find meaning for facts instead of speculation and myth.

---

[6] Edward Gibbon, *The Decline and Fall of the Roman Empire* (New York: Macmillan Company, 1914), 328-329.
[7] Barber, *New Knighthood*, 317.

Much Templar study has been tangential to research on larger subjects such as the history of the Crusades, the Capetians, and the Church. The French King Philip IV, also known as "The Fair" (named like many other Capetian monarchs because of his appearance, not because of his judiciousness), has been seen as a man harboring many different identities such as ambitious monarch, defender of the faith, and greedy tyrant. Pope Clement V has been seen as a reformer, a puppet, and a cannibal. And lastly, the Templars have been viewed through recent historiography as heretics, martyrs, and objects of betrayal. These contrasting views represent historiography that largely pivots on the single event of the Templar suppression. Views often reflect time, location, and research interests.

In looking at the motive for Philip's "destruction" of the Templars, historian Joseph Strayer suggested that "the most obvious and partially true answer is that he was short of money."[8] This motive is a common theme among most historians of the era. Ironically, Strayer concluded that Philip may have overestimated the wealth of the Templars, and most of the property they did possess he was forced to concede to the Knights Hospitaller.[9] What he does not admit was that Clement V did show some backbone in his efforts to transfer Templar property to the Hospital. Philip is also shown as a champion of the Church, continuing his cleansing of the Church that he had begun with the removal of Boniface; Strayer suggests that perhaps Philip, "a thoroughly pious man... took the accusations [of heresy] seriously."[10] However, Strayer does concede that Philip's removal of a top councilor,

---

[8] Joseph Strayer, *The Reign of Philip the Fair* (Princeton: Princeton University Press, 1980).
[9] Ibid., 288.
[10] Ibid.

7

who he had known would disagree with the guilt of the Templars, might show that he had other motives.[11] Strayer is unnecessarily harsh on Clement and largely ignores the trial evidence.

Historian Alan Forey took a much different approach in 1992 when he published his book *The Military Orders: From the Twelfth to the Early Fourteenth Centuries.* Forey, in writing on the Military Orders, the Knights of the Temple, the Knights of the Hospital, and the Knights Teutonic, takes a much different view on why the Templars collapsed. In 1291 the last Templar stronghold in Syria, the city of Acre, fell to the Saracens. As the Templars fled the Holy Land to their island refuge on Cyprus, Forey claimed that the "original function of military orders … was no longer being actively pursued."[12] This original vocation of protecting the pilgrimage to the Holy Land, specifically defending the lands which had been captured in the previous crusades, was now futile and impossible without a new crusade to recapture a foothold in the east. Forey argues that the Holy Land was a "cause which had lasted too long,"[13] and perhaps he would agree with Historian Robert Fawtier that the old Christendom has passed. Nevertheless he disagrees with the notion that the Templars were a relic of an era long lost, and argues that they did still serve as financiers.[14] Forey claims the Templars gained income as a depository for the wealth of the crusaders. The wealthy, who wished to go off on crusade, could leave their property in the hands of Templars in the West, who would look after land, but also reap the

---

[11] Ibid., 289.
[12] Alan Forey, *The Military Orders: From the Twelfth to the Early Fourteenth Centuries* (Toronto: University of Toronto Press, 1992), 239.
[13] Ibid., 241.
[14] Robert Fawtier, *The Capetian Kings of France: Monarchy and Nation 987-1328* (New York: St. Martin's Press, 1978).

benefits (a form of interest) while in possession of it.[15] Forey enumerates many financial tools available to the Templars. Templars participated in money lending not only to businessmen but most significantly to kings. The Aragonese kings and Philip IV were known borrowers of the Templar coin; Philip IV had placed them in charge of the royal treasury of the French Kingdom.

Templar Historian Malcolm Barber's book on *The Trial of the Templars* was the first definitive work on the judicial processes themselves. It offers a wealth of information, trial documents, and witness confessions, using a tremendous amount of evidence to support its arguments. Unfortunately, from the beginning his book manifests a bias in favor of the Templars. As long as this is acknowledged, the reader can see though the lines. Barber also has a presentist perspective, as he explains in a preface;

> I wrote this book for two main reasons. Firstly, because the trial of the Templars was an affair of considerable importance in the middle ages which has been unjustly neglected by historians writing in English, and secondly, because I believe that the event has some relevance to the world of the late twentieth century so many of whose peoples have been, and continue to be, oppressed by regimes which use terror and torture to enforce conformity of thought and action.[16]

One of the most notable revisions is a tendency to judge the confessing Templar knights less harshly. Jim Bradbury's *The Capetians* emphasizes their bravery when facing death. He argues that historians are

---

[15] Ibid., 116.
[16] Malcolm Barber, *The Trial of the Templars,* 2nd ed. (New York: Cambridge University Press, 2006), ix.

wrong to call the Grandmaster James of Molay weak, despite his constant confessions and retractions, because "he was not a coward, and went to a brave death."[17] The most disheartening tale is of the final blow which Philip laid on the Templars. Bradbury states, "There were able and brave Templars who tried to defend the order," but "in 1310 the most cynical card of all was played." Philip IV was tiring of growing Templar resistance and of the many brothers who were prepared to defend the Order so he turned his words into actions. In defiance of Clement, and of papal law, he brutally halted the questions and the "executions began, mainly of those who had denied their original confessions. Fifty-four brothers were burned alive on the edge of the wood of Vincennes. Other burnings quickly followed... This marked the end of any attempt to defend the order. It was a cruel, cynical, and effective move."[18]

When the papal archives were returned to Rome from France after the Napoleonic era, the unfortunate treasure trove of historical information was carried by wagon and forced to face the elements. Upon its arrival, the history of the Avignon Papacy (more commonly known as the Babylonian Captivity), including the Archives of Clement V, was placed in a disheveled and unorganized fashion back within the Papal Archives in the Vatican. Fortunately, Vatican paleographer Barbara Frale was able to find, in September 2001, a misplaced article of parchment. In the archival box Avignonese 48, which was marked as belonging to Benedict XII, Frale found "some paper fascicles dating back to the reign

---

[17] Jim Bradbury, *The Capetians* (New York: Continuum Books, 2007), 271.
[18] Ibid., 273.

of a former pope, Clement V.[19] In her article in the *Journal of Medieval History*, "The Chinon Chart: Papal Absolution to the Last Templar, Master Jacques de Molay," Frale begins to tell a story similar to that of Barber and Forey.

> The attack [on the Templars] was surely due to the monetary needs of the French king at the beginning of the fourteenth century, especially because of the war against England, which had exhausted his revenue; the same maneuver had already been accomplished against the other rich groups in the kingdom, the Lombard bankers and the Jews, who were arrested and had their property confiscated.[20]

Because of Frale's findings, the Roman Catholic Church officially stated its view that Clement's suppression was unfounded, and has documented the reasons for this conclusion in the *Processus contra Templarios*, published by the Vatican Secret Archives in 2007. Despite the Roman Catholic Church's new official stance, the debate on the Templar guilt is far from over. Scholars have tended to focus on the dramatic events of the arrest and trials, and to discover the motives of Philip IV. Some, from Dante to today's historians, have claimed that it was Philip's greed which spurred the Templar's suppression. Others have acted as Philip's apologists and attributed the suppression to his own deep piety, handed down from his saintly grandfather Louis IX. The argument has also been taken in new directions by Malcolm Barber and Jonathan Riley-Smith, who looked at the charges themselves, although their opinions differ. It is this approach which offers a chance to systematically analyze the authenticity of the alleged crimes.

---

[19] Barbara Frale, "The Chinon Chart: Papal Absolution to the Last Templar, Master Jacques de Molay" *Journal of Medieval History* 30 (2004): 111.
[20] Ibid., 112.

Studying the charges requires a better understanding of the Templars and their operations. Their dual identity must be re-invoked, to show how the charges relate not just to individual monks or knights but also to the twelfth-century novelty of the warrior-monk.

The 127 charges levied against the Templars were clearly summarized in Clement's bull *Faciens misericordiam*.[21] These consist of the denial of Christ during initiation, idol worship, failing to believe in the sacraments, the belief that the grand master could absolve sins and hear confession, indecent kisses, greed, and secrecy. Most of these charges center on events that allegedly occurred during the "mysterious" Templar initiation ritual. The reason that the initiation ritual is of such concern is that it is the focal point of the accusations of heresy which spurred the suppression of the Order. The denial of Christ, spitting on the crucifix, indecent kissing, idol worship, and homosexuality were all allegedly part of the initiation.

Surprisingly, what we know of the Templar initiation ritual, also called reception, is actually quite detailed due to the surviving Templar *Rule*. The Templar *Rule* is a canon for the warrior-monks which defines their daily life. The *Rule* is not unique to the Templars, as the regulations and rituals it describes were part of a long monastic tradition that the Templars had modified for their specific military needs. Therefore, the Templar *Rule* and its reception ritual can be interpreted and contextualized in light of their monastic sources, such as the *Rule of the Master*, the *Rule of Benedict*, and Cistercian customs.

To help understand the "guilt" of the Templars, it is necessary to look beyond the absolutes of guilt and innocence and find solace in a

---

[21] Barber, *Trial of the Templars*, 202.

lovely shade of grey. By examining the heritage and tradition of Templar monasticism, the initiation ritual, and the charges made at the time of Philip's suppression, it is possible to come to a better understanding of Templar initiation rite and open new discussion on the Templar's guilt. Templar initiation rites did exist. By studying them, it is possible to see how real rituals and symbols might have been pejoratively interpreted by hostile outsiders. The resulting propaganda would lead to the destruction of one of the most powerful institutions in medieval history.

Chapter II

Templar Monasticism: Heritage and Tradition

> He is truly a fearless knight and secure on every side, for his soul is protected by the armor of faith just as his body is protected by armor of steel. He is thus doubly armed and need fear neither demons nor men. Not that he fears death--no, he desires it.
>
> – Bernard of Clairvaux[22]

It is hard to accept that any group with foundations as humble and holy as the Knights Templar could develop over two centuries into the heretical blasphemers who so "shocked" Philip. Before attempting to judge them, however, it is necessary to understand their historical tradition. Charges such as the secrecy of the initiation ritual or the worship of idols would be impossible to analyze without understanding monastic reverence for holy icons and relics. To judge the charges of illicit kisses and defamation of the cross would be impossible without first understanding the *Rule* of the Templars. Also, confession of sins within the chapter and the absolution abilities of the grand master would be impossible to understand without knowledge of the Order's structure. Therefore, an analysis of the foundation and heritage of Templar

---

[22] Bernard of Clairvaux, "In Praise of the New Knighthood," trans. Conrad Greenia, in *Bernard of Clairvaux: Treatises III: On Grace and Free Choice, In Praise of the New Knighthood*, Cistercian Fathers Series, 19 (Collegeville: Cistercian Publications, 1977), 127-145.

traditions must be made in order to see their connection with their monastic forefathers and to understand the practices that, hostilely interpreted, could give rise to such great scandal.

Foundation and Purpose

After the success of the first crusade, Christians flocked to the Holy Land to visit the sacred sites and relics of their faith. The Latin Church of Jerusalem made it a "prime objective" to restore the great shrines and pilgrimage destinations.[23] According to crusade chronicler Fulcher of Chartres, the route to Jerusalem after landing at the port of Jaffa was dangerous for pilgrims during the early reign of King Baldwin I.[24] Jaffa, the only Latin port in the early years of the Kingdom, was not the best starting point by which to embark to Jerusalem. An English pilgrim named Saewulf chronicles his journey to Jerusalem from Jaffa in 1102-03,

> [It was] a journey of two days, by a mountainous road, very rough, and dangerous on account of the Saracens, who lie in wait in the caves of

---

[23] Jonathan Riley-Smith, *The Crusades: A Short History* (New Haven: Yale University Press, 1987), 43. See Bernard Hamilton's "Rebuilding Zion: The Holy Places of Jerusalem in the Twelfth Century," in *Renaissance and Renewal in Christian History: Papers Read at the Fifteenth Summer Meeting and Sixteenth Winter Meeting of the Ecclesiastical History Society,* ed. Derek Baker, Studies in Church History 14 (Oxford: Basil Blackwell, 1977.), 105-115.

[24] See Fulcher of Chartres, *A History of the Expedition to Jerusalem, 1095-1127,* trans. F.R. Ryan (Knoxville: University of Tennessee Press, 1969).

the mountains to surprise those less capable of resisting by the smallness of their company, or the weary, who may chance to lag behind their companions. At one moment, you see them on every side; at another they are altogether invisible, as may be witnessed by anybody traveling there. Numbers of human bodies lie scattered in the way, and by the wayside, torn to pieces by wild beasts.[25]

Russian Abbot Daniel also wrote about the dangers facing pilgrims during his pilgrimage to the Holy Land in 1106-1107. He states that while traveling from Jerusalem to Ascalon,

> There are plenty of springs at this place, near to which pilgrims come to rest for the night in great fear, for the place is deserted, and not far from the town of Ascalon, whence the Saracens issue and massacre the pilgrims on their way; there is thus much to be feared from this place to the point at which one enters the mountains.[26]

Much of the increased safety of the pilgrimage roads after the 1120's is due to the Templars.[27] In 1119, Hugh of Payens and Godfrey of Saint-Omer co-founded the Knights Templar with a few companions in order to protect the pilgrimage routes to Jerusalem.[28] There are no contemporary accounts of the founding of the order which can be seen as definitive. The best attempt at establishing a founding date of the Knights

---

[25] Saewulf, " The Travels of Saewulf," in *The Crusades: A Reader*, ed. S.J. Allen and Emilie Amt (Peterborough: Broadview Press, 2003), 101.
[26] Abbot Daniel. "The Pilgrimage of the Russian Abbot Daniel in the Holy Land," in *Library of the Palestine Pilgrims' Test Society*, ed. C.W.Wilson (London: Hanover Square, 1895), 9.
[27] For more information on the Templar's strategy in protecting pilgrimage roads, see: Denys Pringle. "Templar Castles on the Road to the Jordan." In *The Military Orders*: vol. 2, *Welfare and Warfare*, ed. H. Nicholson (Aldershot: Ashgate Publishing, 1998), 89-109.
[28] Barber, *New Knighthood*, 9.

Templar was made by Malcolm Barber who after taking account for the "French practice of beginning the year on 25 March", decided that the date must range from the end of 1119 to early 1120.[29] By protecting the pilgrims, the knights gained the gratitude of King Baldwin II of Jerusalem, who granted them a section of his palace at the Al-Aqsa mosque (known to the crusaders as the *Templum Solomonis*), located on the Temple Mount. This clearly indicates that Baldwin endorsed their role and purpose. The Temple Mount soon became the headquarters of the Order, known as the Poor Knights of the Temple of Solomon. With much renovation and alleged excavation, they made the Temple Mount their home. After the fall of Jerusalem in 1187, Acre became the headquarters. To assist their mission, the Templars were granted fortresses along roads and pilgrimage sites. They built castles to maintain the defenses of the routes. As their property and numbers grew, their roles shifted to protecting the entire Kingdom of Jerusalem, not just the pilgrims.

Much of the early Order's history is known from the chronicle of William of Tyre, who wrote *The Foundation of the Order of the Knights Templar* decades later. He labeled Hugh and Geoffrey as "noble men of knightly rank, religious men, devoted to God and fearing him... promised to live in perpetuity as regular canons, without possessions, under vows of chastity and obedience."[30] These are the traditional monastic vows cherished by Latin monasticism for centuries. Because the

---

[29] Ibid.

[30] William of Tyre, *Historia rerum in partibus transmarinis gestarum*, XII, 7th ed. *Patrologia Latina* 201: 526-27, translated by James Brundage, *The Crusades: A Documentary History* (Milwaukee, WI: Marquette University Press, 1962), 70-73. A full translation of the William's history can be found in: William of Tyre, *A History of Deeds Done beyond the Sea, by William, Archbishop of Tyre*, trans. Emily Atwater Babcock and A.C. Krey (New York: Columbia University Press, 1943).

Templars were living communally in their "Temple" accommodations, observing vows of chastity and poverty, they would have been seen by their contemporaries as analogous to "reformed canons." Perhaps some of the traditions formed in their early years could have made an imprint on the later Templar *Rule*.

The Templars were maintaining their pilgrimage routes and their headquarters at the al Aqsa mosque in 1126, when Hugh of Payens began a recruiting tour through Europe.[31] Under orders from King Baldwin II of Jerusalem, Hugh had attached himself to the royal embassy which was traveling west to Anjou to offer the king's daughter Melisende's hand to Fulk of Anjou for marriage. Baldwin II had no male heirs, and establishing a succession was a priority. Hugh of Payens, now Master of the Temple, set off to recruit for the east, as well as obtain papal confirmation of his order, already in process due to an 1126 letter to Bernard of Clairvaux from Baldwin II himself.[32]

Benedictine and Cistercian Influence through the Hands of Bernard

Bernard of Clairvaux was the most influential monk of the twelfth century.[33] When he entered the monastery of Cîteaux in 1111, it was a small struggling community. At the time of his death in 1153, there were 343 Cistercian houses. Giles Constable writes of Bernard, "In the second quarter of the century, no one could touch the influence of Bernard of Clairvaux... one of the few figures of his time (or, indeed, of

---

[31] Barber, *New Knighthood*, 12.
[32] Ibid.
[33] For a biography of Bernard see: Adriaan H. Bredero, *Bernard of Clairvaux: Between Cult and History* (Grand Rapids: Eerdmans Publishing, 1996).

any time) who was equally important as a writer and as a man of affairs."[34]

Bernard would have considered himself part of a monastic reform movement, marked by the shift to the white habit, the mark of the Cistercian order to which he belonged. He envisioned himself as an angel of God, not merely a man, and his habit reflected this.[35] The idea that the monastic habit embodied angelic symbolism was not new. Pope Boniface IV and Peter Damian had both described the monk's habit as having six wings like the heavenly cherubim, "two on the head, two to right and left, and two in front and behind."[36] With the habit of the Cistercian Order in the time of Bernard of Clairvaux being white, in contrast to the traditional Cluniac black, the argument was even more compelling.

Bernard's idea of a monk could be due to his background and lineage. He was born into a knightly family. According to William of St. Thierry, writing c.1140, Bernard's father "Tescelin, was a member of an ancient and knightly family, fearing God and scrupulously just. Even when engaged in holy war he plundered and destroyed no one; he contented himself with his worldly possessions, of which he had an abundance, and used them in all manner of good works."[37] Bernard chose

---

[34] Giles Constable, *The Reformation of the Twelfth Century* (New York: Cambridge University Press, 2002), 108.

[35] Giles Constable, "The Ceremonies and Symbolism of Entering Religious Life and Taking the Monastic Habit from Fourth to the Twelfth Century," in *Segni e riti nella Chiesa altomedievale occidentale*, 2 vols. Settimane di studio del Centro italiano, di studi sull alto Medioevo, 33 (Spoleto: CISAM, 1981), vol. 2, 801.

[36] Ibid., 818.

[37] Frederic Austin Ogg, ed., *A Source Book of Mediaeval History: Documents Illustrative of European Life and Institutions from the German Invasions to the Renaissance* (New York: Cooper Square Publishers, 1972), 251.

a path of monastic life at the monastery of Cîteaux. William writes in his *Life of St. Bernard,*

> Such were the holy beginnings of the monastic life of that man of God. It is impossible to any one who has not been imbued as he with the spirit of God to recount the illustrious deeds of his career, and his angelic conduct, during his life on earth. He entered the monastery poor in spirit, still obscure and of no fame, with the intention of there perishing in the heart and memory of men, and hoping to be forgotten and ignored like a lost vessel. But God ordered it otherwise, and prepared him as a chosen vessel, not only to strengthen and extend the monastic order, but also to bear His name before kings and peoples to the ends of the earth.[38]

When Bernard received word of this new Templar Order from King Baldwin II of Jerusalem, he would naturally have been interested in the *Pauperes Commilitones Christi Templique Solomonici*. When Hugh of Payens arrived at the Council of Troyes in 1128/29, Bernard immediately began to envision the structure of the Templars in his own image of the *milites christi*.

The Council of Troyes was the climax of Hugh of Payens' European tour.[39] After visiting England, Scotland, and the many territories of France, he had acquired donations and patrimonial land throughout Latin Christendom, establishing a strong base of operations as well as facilities for permanent recruitment in the west. When he arrived at the council, he gave a speech which described the simple precepts of the order, and its communal identity under the jurisdiction of the Master,

---

[38] Ibid., 251-258.
[39] Barber, *New Knighthood*, 14.

who answered only to the Patriarch of Jerusalem.[40] During the Council, Hugh and Bernard constructed the official Latin *Rule of the Templars*. Bernard is praised twice in the Templar *Rule* itself for participating in its creation. The scribe writes, "Therefore I, Jean Michel, to whom was entrusted and confided that divine office, by the grace of God served as humble scribe of the present document by order of the council and of the venerable father Bernard, abbot of Clairvaux."[41] Clearly Bernard is on equal footing with the entire council. Later in the *Rule*, Bernard is listed last of the religious, "whose words the aforementioned praised liberally."[42]

After completion of the *Rule* at the council, Pope Honorius II gave the Templars papal sanction, officially forming the Templars and legitimizing their dual identity in the eyes of the Church. Bernard continued to promote the Order. His treatise *In Praise of the New Knighthood* presented the new ideal of powerful warrior-monks. Hereafter, *milites Christi* would fight not only spiritually but also physically. He writes,

> This is, I say, a new kind of knighthood and one unknown to the ages gone by. It ceaselessly wages a twofold war both against flesh and blood and against a spiritual army of evil in the heavens. When someone strongly resists a foe in the flesh, relying solely on the strength of the flesh, I would hardly remark it, since this is common enough. And when war is waged by spiritual strength against vices or demons, this, too, is nothing remarkable, praiseworthy as it is, for the world is full of monks. But when the one sees a man

---

[40] Ibid., 15.
[41] Judi Upton-Ward, trans. *The Rule of the Templars: The French Text of the Rule of the Order of the Knights Templar* (Rochester: Boydell and Brewer, 2008), 20.
[42] Ibid., 21.

powerfully girding himself with both swords and nobly marking his belt, who would not consider it worthy of all wonder, the more so since it has been hitherto unknown? He is truly a fearless knight and secure on every side, for his soul is protected by the armor of faith just as his body is protected by armor of steel. He is thus doubly armed and need fear neither demons nor men. Not that he fears death--no, he desires it. Why should he fear to live or fear to die when for him to live is Christ, and to die is gain? Gladly and faithfully he stands for Christ, but he would prefer to be dissolved and to be with Christ, by far the better thing.[43]

Bernard and the Templars changed the dynamic of monasticism and the identity of the *milites Christi* forever. Regardless of how revolutionary this change had been, it was not without strong thematic borrowings from earlier monastic history. For the purposes of studying the initiation ritual of the Templars, it is imperative to recognize that the Latin *Rule of the Templars* borrowed from the *Rule of Benedict*, which itself used the *Rule of the Master* as a source. At points it seems Bernard and the writers must have copied verbatim from the *Rule of Benedict* and definitely used it as a basis for the monastic life and reception for the Templars. Gustav Schnürer has identified 30 clauses in the *Rule* which are taken literally from the *Rule of Benedict*.[44] Also, the *Rule* gives the Templars one of the strongest physical connections to Bernard and his Cistercian brethren, the white habit.

---

[43] Bernard, "In Praise," 127-145.

[44] Gustav Schnürer. *Die ursprüngliche Templeregel: Vergleich der lateinischen und der französischen Ausgabe der Regel* (Freiburg im Breisgau: Herder, 1903), 57, n.3.

The Evolution of the Templar Rule

The first official Templar *Rule*, the Latin *Rule*, resulted from the Council of Troyes in 1129. As the order exploded in size, wealth, and popularity, the Latin *Rule*'s original 168 precepts grew to encompass the 686 precepts found in the French *Rule* written between 1257 and 1268.[45] Known as the *Retrais*, the additional precepts following the Latin *Rule* (relabeled the "Primitive *Rule*" in the new manuscripts), included sections on hierarchical statutes, penances, conventual life, the holding of ordinary chapters and most importantly, the reception into the Order. The *Retrais* were not circulated widely to the lower echelons of the order and were hidden from the public at large. However the members knew these rules through readings during chapter and reception by the master of the commandery. Judi Upton Ward, translator of the French version of the *Rule* and the *Retrais* into English, points out that precept 326 forbade all brothers from carrying the *Rule* or the *Retrais* unless ordered by the higher officials, because of a previous situation in which squires had disclosed this information to secular men.[46] It was necessary to prevent the *Rule* from falling into enemy hands because as Matthew Bennett in "*La Régle du Temple* as a Military Manual, or How to Deliver a Cavalry Charge" argues, much of the *Rule* can be seen as a military manual for the Order.

Therefore it can be suggested, and has been by Vatican scholar Barbara Frale, that in reality there might have been some ceremonies where the higher echelons of the Order responsible for the *Rule* were not in attendance. If a new recruit was being initiated, it may not have been

---

[45] Upton-Ward, *French Rule,* 16.
[46] Ibid., 92.

23

done by following the official guidelines, and the *Rule* may not have been read to the postulant as required.[47] Although this would not have been the case in the larger commanderies, such as Paris or Acre, where high officials would always be present, the smaller isolated commanderies may not have possessed the *Rule* in its entirety. Frale suggests that they would have had excerpts from sections which they would have needed, such as that on reception. Evidence supporting this is in the structure of the surviving French texts. The reception ritual itself fits awkwardly with its surrounding text, and feels more like an appendix. Of the five remaining manuscripts of the *Rule*, Malcolm Barber claims that the one known as the "Catalan *Rule*," used by the master in Catalonia and Aragon, shows more wear and tear in the reception section of the *Rule* than in any other.[48] Therefore, it can be presumed that the *Rule* was used, read and practiced within the initiation ritual of the order. The Catalan *Rule* has been dated to after 1268 and possibly after 1273, because of its mention of the loss of the Templar castle of Baghras, so the *Rule* must have been widely used in the decades immediately before the suppression of the Order.[49]

Structure and Hierarchies

Although a look at the hierarchies of the Templars is tangential to this project, certain structural aspects need to be introduced in order to put the initiation rituals in context. This ritual itself would occur in a Templar property, which could be a castle, church, or small building. These are generally called commanderies and were the basic structural

---

[47] Frale, *The Templars,* 166.

[48] Barber, *New Knighthood,* 184.

[49] Judi Upton-Ward, *The Catalan Rule of the Templars* (Woodbridge: The Boydell Press, 2003), xii.

units within the Templar Order.[50] These commanderies were typical of monasteries in that they were houses where the brethren of the Order lived and maintained chapter. In them the Templar brothers normally spent their daily lives. The commanderies housed refectories where the members ate their food communally and in near silence during readings from the Gospels and other texts.[51]

Commanderies had an economic and administrative function meant to support the whole order. Contemporaries marveled at the vast land holdings of the Templars. For example, look at the property held by the commandery of Baugy in Caen. A detailed inventory taken by the royal legates of Philip IV as they came to survey the commandery of Baugy on the 13th of October, 1307 shows its wealth. The livestock alone consisted of thirty-one head of cattle, two oxen, one-hundred sheep, one-hundred and eighty ewes and lambs, ninety-eight pigs and sows, eight mares and a few pack horses.[52] A significant parcel of farmland, documented at seventy-seven acres, was maintained by twenty-seven servants who might also be considered property.[53] The furnishings and vestments surveyed were lavish and included silverware, silk cloths and garments.[54] Baugy was not unique. Four other houses within its *baiuliae* show similar holdings.[55]

---

[50] Jonathan Riley-Smith, "The Structures of the Orders of the Temple and the Hospital." In *The Medieval Crusade*, ed. Susan J. Ridyard (Woodbridge: Boydell Press, 2004), 126.

[51] "The Latin Rule of 1129," in Barber and Bate, *Templars: Selected Sources*, 37.

[52] "Inventories of Templar Property in Normandy" (13 October 1307), in Barber and Bate, *Templars: Selected Sources*, 191.

[53] Ibid., 192.

[54] Ibid., 193.

[55] Ibid., 191-201.

For administrative purposes, these commanderies would were grouped into *baiuliae*, consisting of traditional commanderies as well as other land holdings and houses.[56] This can be shown by the way some commanderies house members of other houses.[57] Each commandery would be run by its commander or provincial master, a role which would be filled by knights, sergeants, or priests.[58] To administer multiple commanderies and *baiuliae*, provinces existed: Tripoli, Jerusalem, Antioch, France, England, Poitou, Aragon, Portugal, Apulia, and Hungary were provinces each led by a grand commander who was in charge of coordinating their efforts.[59] The Templars also had a headquarters: first in Jerusalem, until its fall to Saladin in 1187; then in Acre until its fall in 1291; and then on Cyprus. Here the highest members of the Templars ran the order at large.[60] At the head of the hierarchy was the grand master, a man with no superiors except for Rome and God. He was elected by the majority of his peers, but, as in other monastic communities, the majority at times would be simply "the sounder and purer part of them."[61]

Within the Order itself there were many types of members. The Templar knights were nobly born and wore the white habit. The sergeant brothers were the most numerous members, and wore a habit of black or

---

[56] Riley-Smith, "Structures," 127.

[57] Ibid.

[58] Ibid.

[59] Barber, *Trial of the Templars*, 13.

[60] For more information on the hierarchies of the Knights Templar, as well as the best prosopographical database of Templar officers, see Jochen Burgtorf, *The Central Convent of Hospitallers and Templars: History, Organization, and Personnel (1099/1120-1310)* (Boston: Brill, 2008).

[61] "Omne datum optimum" (29 March 1139), in Barber and Bate, *Templars: Selected Sources,* 59-64.

brown. Also, at times the Order would enlist temporary brothers, who could be hired soldiers or knights. Quite different however were the priest brothers. Not only was their initiation different, but according to the *Rule*, they were the only Templars not allowed to fight. The knights, sergeants, and priests formed the three basic groups of the Templars, who all lived together in unity. During the initiation ritual, the head of the commandery as well as the Templar priest, might be holding the chapter, while the rest of the knights and brothers would sit in attendance. The hierarchies and structure of the way in which chapter is held leads one to believe that hazing could take place, but perhaps understanding the sacred of the initiation rite can further explain the meaning of the ritual itself.

Chapter III

The Templar Initiation Ritual

If any secular knight, or any other
man, wishes to leave the mass of perdition and
abandon that secular life and choose your
communal life, do not consent to receive him
immediately, for thus said my lord St Paul:
Probate spiritus si ex Deo sunt. That is to say:
'Test the soul to see if it comes from God.'
Rather, if the company of the brothers is to be
granted to him, let the Rule be read to him,
and if he wishes to studiously obey the
commandments of the Rule, and if it pleases
the Master and the brothers to receive him, let
him reveal his wish and desire before all the
brothers assembled in chapter and let him
make his request with a pure heart.

– The Templar *Rule*[62]

Christianity places a particular importance on the transformation
of man through the rituals of baptism. This transformation is a
metaphysical "conversion" of one's soul into a new state of existence.[63]
Entering religious life also continues the rituals of baptism inasmuch as it
attempts, to transform the initiate into a new being for a second time. It is

---

[62] Upton-Ward, *French Rule.*
[63] For more on the connection between baptism and conversion, see
Gerhart B. Ladner, *The Idea of Reform: Its Impact on Christian Thought
and Action in the Age of the Fathers* (Cambridge: Harvard Univ. Press,
1959), 168-169, 194-199, 127-138.

important to look at the origins of these rituals, and their symbolic nature pertaining to initiation.

Initiation rituals originated as quite ancient forms of ceremonial rites of passage. Arnold van Gennep studied many different forms in his *Les rites de passage* (1909). He established different categories of rites of passage such as birth or marriage, but most importantly that of the initiation rite. He argues that most initiation rites consist of a three step sequence of "rites of separation, transition, and incorporation."[64] These three stages correlate directly with the Templar initiation rite.

It is also important to understand the primitive desire for initiation ritual to understand why a Templar initiate would want to go through the process. Mircea Eliade has done tremendous work on understanding the nature of the need for ritual ceremonies. He argues in his book *The Sacred & Profane: The Nature of Religion* that "In a word, it may be said that human existence attains completion through a series of "passage rites," in short, by successive initiations."[65] He continues to analyze how that passage offers a religious man a "veritable ontological mutation."[66] This change is not simply of a man mutating to another form. Eliade argues that man can become one with the superhuman. He writes,

> This means: (1) one does not become a complete man until one has passed beyond, and in some sense abolished, "natural" humanity, for initiation is reducible to a paradoxical, supernatural experience of

---

[64] Arnold van Gennep, *The Rites of Passage* trans. Monika B. Vizedom and Gabrielle L. Caffee (Chicago: University of Chicago Press, 1960), 96.
[65] Mircea Eliade, *The Sacred & the Profane: The Nature of Religion,* trans. Willard Trask (New York: HBJ Publishers, 1987), 181.
[66] Ibid.

death and resurrection or of second birth; (2) initiation rites, entailing ordeals and symbolic death and resurrection, were instituted by gods, culture heroes, or mythical ancestors; hence these rites have a superhuman origin, and by performing them the novice imitates a superhuman, divine action. It is important to note this, for it shows once again that religious man *wants to be other* than he finds himself on the "natural" level and undertakes to *make himself* in accordance with the ideal image revealed to him by myths. Primitive man undertakes to attain a religious ideal of humanity, and his effort already contains the germs of all the ethics later elaborated in modern societies.[67]

For the Templars, initiation was, as monastic tradition would declare, a new baptism. A papal decree attributed to Pope Gregory I was suggested by Giles Constable to have been written in Italy around the middle of the eleventh century. It shows monastic profession as a second baptism.[68] The decree states, "Therefore he has been baptized for a second time and cleansed [according to the judgment of the holy fathers] from all the sins [of his former life]."[69] There has been debate on whether taking the monastic habit constituted a second baptism, but the alleged papal decree of Gregory I, as well as Saint Peter Damian, are very conclusive. Peter Damian clearly mocks his target, in his thirty-eighth letter, by posing the question, "Have you never read that a vow to lead the monastic life is a second baptism?"[70]

Scholastic theologian Saint Thomas Aquinas would agree with Gregory and Damian. He wrote in his definitive *Summa Theologica,*

[67] Ibid., 187-188.
[68] Constable, "The Ceremonies and Symbolism," 795.
[69] Ibid.
[70] Peter Damian, *Letter* 38, trans. Owen J. Blum, *Peter Damian Letters 31-60,* The Fathers of the Church: Mediaeval Continuation, 2 (Washington DC: The Catholic University of America Press, 1990), 92.

Moreover it may be reasonably stated that also by entrance into religion a man obtains remission of all his sins. For if by giving alms a man may forthwith satisfy for his sins, according to (Daniel 4:24), "Redeem thou thy sins with alms," much more does it suffice to satisfy for all his sins that a man devote himself wholly to the divine service by entering religion, for this surpasses all manner of satisfaction, even that of public penance, according to the Decretals (XXXIII, qu. i, cap. Admonere) just as a holocaust exceeds a sacrifice, as Gregory declares (Hom. xx in Ezech.). Hence we read in the Lives of the Fathers (vi, 1) that by entering religion one receives the same grace as by being baptized. And yet even if one were not thereby absolved from all debt of punishment, nevertheless the entrance into religion is more profitable than a pilgrimage to the Holy Land, as regards the advancement in good, which is preferable to absolution from punishment.[71]

It has been concluded by Giles Constable that, "there can be no doubt that entry to monastic life was almost universally regarded in the Middle Ages as truly a second baptism or regeneration."[72]

Knights Templar initiates were taking the monastic habit as Benedict, Bernard, and their own heroes Hugh of Payens and other brothers had before them. In taking the habit, they abolished their "natural humanity" by renouncing the world, and by vowing the three monastic vows of poverty, chastity, and obedience. By wanting to become "other," the Templar initiates moved themselves to a higher plane according to the mythos described in Bernard's *In Praise of the New Knighthood* and the legends of Templar glory they had heard in their

---

[71] "*Summa Theologica:* The Entrance into Religious Life (Secunda Secundae Partis, Q. 189)" *New Advent.* 2008.
http://www.newadvent.org/summa/3189.htm (accessed May 11, 2010).
[72] Constable, "The Ceremonies and Symbolism," 800.

lifetime. As the Templars went through the initiation, they went through an ordeal which bonded them with fellow brothers. They shared a common experience, as well as the mystery. Eliade argues that in initiation he "who has experienced the mysteries, *is he who knows*."[73] Initiation rituals necessarily involve elements of mystery and secrecy.

In its primitive form, Eliade argues, the initiation rite consists of strong rituals. These are performed by first separating the initiate from the others, in a solitary place. This is to symbolize death or the return to the fetal state within the womb.[74] Here the initiate begins to undergo the torture, or hazing. Eventually the initiate will leave his "womb" and be reborn with a new identity able to receive his secret knowledge, and his ritual markings.[75] For the Templars, this will be a moment of hearing the Order's history, successes and failures, as well as the taking of the habit.

In many modern day Christian churches, ritual has been deemphasized. Renowned anthropologist Mary Douglas reminds us that, "With every new century we become heirs to a longer and more vigorous anti-ritualist tradition."[76] But ritual and ceremony were very important within the medieval church. Specifically in monastic life, Giles Constable reminds us that,

> From the moment when a child was brought to a monastery as an oblate or when a postulant came to the gate requesting admission their behavior followed a customary routine or written code which varied in detail from community to community but always had the double purpose both of fostering unity and harmony

---

[73] Ibid., 189.

[74] Ibid.

[75] Ibid., 191.

[76] Mary Douglas, *Purity and Danger* (Harmondsworth: Penguin Books, 1970), 77-78, 83.

among the members and of relating their lives to the broad spiritual ends of the life of religion.[77]

Rituals throughout time have been used for many different purposes, such as remembering the dead, reenacting the past, or teaching lessons. Rituals can be used also for coming-of-age ceremonies, religious devotion, and marriage. In the monastery, ritual and symbolism function by connecting with the past, "bridging the gap between past and present", reminding participants of what has come before, and what shall be.[78] Rituals shaped every part of monastic life from initiation to death. Through repetition these rituals would be known to the monastic members. Someday the new initiate might become the abbot himself, presiding over ceremonies he had experienced years before. This continuity maintained stability, legacy, and tradition amongst brothers who would continue these practices for centuries. However, rituals are in no way absolute. With the creation of new orders such as the Cistercians and the military orders themselves, the monastic life reveals its ability to adapt, change, and reform over time. Giles Constable reminds us that there is an inherent danger in the assumption that all forms of ceremonies maintained their exact meaning and were never modified. He cites as evidence the discarding of liturgical books in the eleventh and twelfth centuries for modified shorter versions within monastic houses.[79]

Certain symbols worn by the Knights Templar, specifically the iconic red cross, had a long and important history within the monastic community. The cross was a beacon of faith, as well as spiritual and physical protection from the demons of this world, and the next. It has

---

[77] Constable, "The Ceremonies and Symbolism," 772-773.
[78] Ibid., 775.
[79] Ibid.

been seen as an "almost universal antidote for the distractions and temptations of monks."[80] Much of this continuity, and respect for tradition and rule can be seen within the Templar's initiation ritual.

The Probationary Year

The monastic tradition established by the *Rule of the Master* and the *Rule of Benedict* flowed through Cistercian hands into the *Rule of the Templars*. This is evident in the Latin *Rule* of 1129, precept 55, titled "The Reception of Secular Knights."

> If any knight from the mass of perdition or any other secular wishes to renounce the world and chooses your community and way of life, entry should not be granted to him immediately, but in accordance with the words of the Apostle: "Test the spirit whether it comes from God', and in that way shall entry be granted him. The Rule should be read to him, and if he obey carefully the precepts of the Rule as set out, then, if the master and brothers are willing to accept him, let all the brothers be assembled so that he can expound to them his desire and his request with a pure heart. Then the term of his probation period should depend totally on the judgment and foresight of the master, taking into consideration the honorable nature of the candidate's life.[81]

The language echoes precept 58: *The Procedure of Accepting Brothers* contained in the *Rule of Saint Benedict*, which itself replicated the *Rule of the Master*. The opening line, as well as apostolic quotation

---

[80] Ibid., 776.

[81] "The Latin Rule of 1129." in Barber and Bate, *Templars: Selected Sources*, 49.

34

from 1st John 4:1 is identical.[82] In the *Rule of Saint Benedict*, the postulant begins with a humble knocking on the door. He is then rebuked, ignored, and tested for patience for four or five days before being allowed entry into the house. The probationary period contained in the Latin *Rule* is used for the purpose of testing the new recruit but does not require the traditional one year, which is specifically outlined in precept 58 of the *Rule of Saint Benedict*. If the duration was at the discretion of the master of that commandery, it could be as short or as long as he determined. However, sometime after the initial Latin *Rule* was written, we see that in the surviving Catalan and French versions all mention of the probationary period was completely removed.

The Battle of Hattin seems a likely catalyst for the dropping of the required probationary year. Most of the eastern Templar force was wiped out, along with most of the army of Jerusalem. Templar Grand Commander Terricus wrote two desperate letters in 1187 and 1188 begging for reinforcements for the east.[83] Recruitment regulations might have been relaxed because of the need for increased manpower. After the loss at Hattin, most of the Templars were executed by Saladin. However, Grand Master Gerard of Ridefort survived, as a captive and bargaining tool for Saladin. As a personal witness to the losses at Hattin, and with the experience of being a Muslim captive, perhaps he had some changes to make when he returned to the Christian ranks after handing over the castle of Gaza to Saladin.[84] With the losses of many members, and after Hattin the subsequent loss of the Templar headquarters at Jerusalem, the

---

[82] Terrence Kardong. *Benedict's Rule: A Translation and Commentary* (Collegeville: The Liturgical Press, 1996), 463. The latin: *Probate spiritus si ex Deo sunt.*
[83] Barber, *New Knighthood*, 115.
[84] Ibid., 116.

new Grand Master would need to quickly replenish the Templar's manpower. Undoubtedly he would have tremendous resources in the West, but would need them fast. The losses at La Forbie in 1244 and during the crusades of St. Louis might have required similar action.

What is known for certain is that the probationary period was dropped by the time the surviving texts were written, sometime between 1257 and 1268. By dropping the probationary period, a major opportunity to test new initiates was lost. More of the burden of testing recruits would now fall on the actual initiation ceremony. Although the catalyst remains uncertain, the changes in the rule have a direct effect on the initiation ceremony. Historically, the use of the one year probationary period has been heavily debated by monks. The anonymous author from Bec of the *Tractatus de professionibus monachorum* mentions that in the past, when the probationary period was in use, joining a monastery was much harder compared to his time.

> Entry for those who were received was not easy, but for some days beforehand they were tested with many different exacting labors, following the apostle's injunction: But try the spirits if they be of God. At that time no one used to be received as easily as they are now.[85]

Peter Damian argues that the year of probation for a new monk to join an order, although mentioned in various rules and used commonly as a step to join many monastic cloisters, was not always necessary. He spoke for hermits who required more flexibility. He argues that it was completely a discretionary tool to be used on the novice. He begins his argument by posing the hypothetical scenario of two recruits, one healthy

---

[85] Constable, *Three Treatises from Bec on the Nature of Monastic Life,* trans. Bernard S. Smith (Toronto: University of Toronto Press, 2008), 33.

and one sick. If a sick man wants to join a monastic order, the probationary period could be too long for him to survive, and would not only be a detriment to his soul but also to the Order which lost the potential benefits of his membership.[86] Peter Damian states that it is physically impossible for the sick to even "fulfill this condition", and that St. Benedict never intended to "shut the door of conversion in the face of the weak and decrepit who cannot rise to bear this burden".[87] He even asks his reader to "scan all the sound histories of antiquity ... and ... you will be unable to come up with even one who was tried by such a long period of probation."[88] Peter Damian clearly feels that long probation was not something which the church fathers and early monks had to endure, and if it is argued that becoming a monk requires the probationary period, then all the aforementioned men would be under scrutiny. The use of the probationary period of one year is not without its purpose. Peter Damian feels that it should rather be used as a "wise precaution against wanderers and ambiguous characters than as an authoritative precept."[89] The abbot should be able to distinguish when encountering a potential novice, whether the man is true of heart and mind. If he is not, the probationary period would give plenty of time to investigate the intentions of the novice. Even the traditional period of one year is challenged, because Peter Damian argues that, "Once you are certain that the spirit of deceit is not present, the probationary period should cease."[90] In particular, if the man is of known virtue within the local community, perhaps no probationary period should be required at all.

---

[86] Peter Damian, *Letter* 38, trans. Blum, 92.
[87] Ibid.
[88] Ibid., 94.
[89] Ibid.
[90] Ibid., 95.

Thomas Aquinas is much stricter when it comes to the probationary period than Peter Damian. Thomas argues in his *Summa* that "The vow of religious profession, for the reason that it binds a man to remain in religion for evermore, has to be preceded by a year of probation."[91] For Aquinas, the seriousness of the lifelong commitment of taking the monastic habit seems to be too important to be something given without any sort of probationary period.

Isolation and Scrutinum

The Templar initiation ceremony starts within the chapter room, where the Master first begins to ask the chapter if any brother sees any issues, or knows anything which would deem the candidate unfit to join the brotherhood. If no one objects, the initiate would be summoned and placed "in a chamber near the chapter, and then he should send two worthy men or three of the oldest of the house, who best know how to indicate what is fitting."[92] This would be the ritualistic womb of Mircea Eliade's rite of passage. After being left in "womb" for some time, the seniors of the house who were charged with this job would begin his "ritualistic torture" or what was called in monastic terms the *scrutinum*.

The *scrutinum*, or more simply the interrogation, was a series of questions which were pressed on the initiate before initiation. Similar to the scrutiny placed on the individual before baptism, they were originally meant to ensure that no one forced the hand of the initiate to join and to also make sure he was free of all worldly obligations such as a wife,

---

[91] "*Summa Theologica*: The Entrance into Religious Life (Secunda Secundae Partis, Q. 189)" *New Advent.* 2008.
http://www.newadvent.org/summa/3189.htm (accessed May 11, 2010).
[92] Upton-Ward, *French Rule,* 168.

slavery, or secret illness. The anonymous author from Bec who wrote the *Tractatus de professionibus* mentions that the *scrutinum* is one of the three basic elements of becoming a monk.[93] The other two are the "taking of the habit", and the monastic "promise" or profession. While the *scrutinum* was in progress within the smaller chamber, the initiate could probably hear the brothers in the main chapter room discussing his worth and purpose. Afterwards, the senior brothers leave the initiate in the chamber and proceed out into the chapter room. Then the *Rule* states that after the senior brothers report to the larger chapter, the master will ask all the brothers, "Do you wish him to be brought on behalf of God? The brothers would then proclaim, "Bring him on behalf of God.'"[94]

The initiate, surely now trembling with fear of what is to come, is then instructed by the same seniors the appropriate way in which to enter the chapter for the first time to request admission to the Order. The *Rule* states that the brother should enter the room, and kneel to the master, hands joined, and should say, "Sire, I am here before God and before you and before the brothers, and ask and request you for the Love of God and our Lady, to welcome me into your company and the favours of the house, as one who wishes to be a serf and slave of the house forever." The master, after acknowledging the request, then preaches to the initiate the burdens of the life of the warrior monk and reminds him that his destination is unknown.

Specifically it mentions that he may be sent to any Templar property. Places mentioned were England, France, Antioch, Acre, Apulia, Sicily, Burgundy and many other exotic locations. Interestingly, this portion of the French *Rule* reveals a change over time. The Catalan *Rule*,

---

[93] Constable, *Three Treatises from Bec,* 22-23.
[94] Ibid.

which as mentioned was written later, merely states, "If you wish to be in one land you will be in another".[95] The change is most likely due to the fact that many of the locales listed in the French *Rule* had been lost by the time the Catalan *Rule* was written.

The initiate is asked once again if, knowing what he now knows of the burden of the Templars, he is ready and willing to become one. If the initiate answers yes, he is immediately told to go outside the chapter house and "pray to God that he advise you."[96] Here we see the final deliberation between the master and the brothers on the initiate, while he prays and ponders nervously what is being said about him inside. If they choose to accept him, the master will say, "Do you wish him to be brought on behalf of God?", and the brothers will repeat, "Bring him on behalf of God." One of the seniors would then fetch him to prepare for reception.

Reception

As the initiate enters the chapter, he once again kneels, with hands joined, and asks again for reception. The master responds, "Have you considered well, good brother, that you wish to be a serf and slave of the Order, and leave behind your own will forever to do another's? And do you wish to suffer all the hardships which are established in the house and carry out all the orders which you have been given?" It is here that the initiate finally makes the monastic promise to the house. In some

---

[95] Upton-Ward, *Catalan Rule,* 33.
[96] Ibid., 35.

situations this may have been a verbal profession, an actual written statement, or a signed letter, given to the master himself.[97]

Thus in the name of God, Mary, the Saints, and all the brothers of the Temple, the initiate becomes a brother, and all the favors, benefits, and burdens of the Order, are now his. The master then places upon him the habit, the iconic monastic cloak, which, if he was a knight, would be white, or, if he was a sergeant, black or brown. Fulfilling his reception, the initiate would recite Psalm 133, which states how good and pleasant it is when brothers live together in unity. For brethren who were not literate, memorizing this psalm in Latin might have been a challenge.

The new brother is then raised by the master, and, as stated by the *Rule*, is to "kiss him on the mouth." The kiss, which was commonly bestowed on neophytes in ordination and baptism, was not homosexual in nature, and is similar to the kiss of peace. In many cases, this practice continues today in modern monastic initiations, such as the Order of Saint Benedict, where the initiate exchanges the kiss of peace with each brother, asking for his prayers.[98] After the formalities of the ritual are over, the master then says, "Good brother, Our Lord has led you to your desire and has placed you in such fine company as is the Knighthood of the Temple." He continues to caution the new recruit on the struggles of maintaining the habit, and says, "We will tell you some of those things which we remember of the failings of the house and the habit."

The new brother is given eight long speeches on the instructions of the Order, on how to live the monastic life, and on all the ways in which he could be expelled from the Order. These lessons reveal strong

---

[97] Upton-Ward, *French Rule,* 81.
[98] Kardong, *Benedict,* 476.

thematic elements of the Knights Templar, specifically their education methods. Throughout their history of nearly two centuries, Templars had many successes and many failures. They had learned what worked in war, business, and monastic lifestyle, and what did not. Therefore, in the Catalan *Rule*, when over half, nearly 140 precepts out of the 206 in the entire rule, are specific examples of failures of house and habit, we can see the importance the Templars placed on tradition, and the handing down of information through the example of other knights. More details of these will be explained further when discussing the accusations against the Templars, but each major charge listed in the charges of Philip IV is mentioned in the Templar *Rule* itself as having occurred at one time within the Order.

Chapter IV

Hostile Perceptions and Accusations

> ... a bitter thing, a lamentable thing, a
> thing horrible to contemplate, terrible to hear,
> a heinous crime, an execrable evil, an
> abominable deed, a hateful disgrace, a
> completely inhuman thing, indeed remote
> from all humanity.
>
> –Philip IV on the crimes of the
> Templars[99]

Friday the 13th of October, 1307, King Philip IV of France stunned Latin Christendom by beginning his assault on the Knights Templar. He confiscated the immense property of the Order and arrested the knights and sergeants throughout all of France.[100] The Templars were charged with many heresies including the denial of Christ, homosexuality, and idol worship. They immediately fell victim to Philip the Fair's papal inquisitors. Even the grandmaster of the Templars, James of Molay, was swept up.[101] Templar property was divided amongst Philip's loyal subjects for protection. Although the Templars had been facing criticism since the beginning of their history, their deeds, glory,

---

[99] "Philip IV's *Order for the Arrests*" (14 September 1307), in Barber and Bate, *Templars: Selected Sources*, 244.
[100] Barber, *Trial of the Templars*, 1.
[101] Ibid.

and power had protected them. However, with the loss of the Holy Land, and the fall of Acre in 1291, their reputation and abilities no longer sufficed. Proposals were made to amalgamate the military orders, and while the Templars and Hospitallers were making preparations for their next big moves, plots and intrigue were forming as early as 1305, led by Philip IV of France.

Early Criticisms

Despite the Knights Templar's humble beginnings, the order in the twelfth and thirteenth centuries became associated with wealth, and power. When the trials began, hostile testimony in the west was seen strongly in England, where "the Templars would have been known mainly as wealthy and privileged landowners, [and] there was a considerable amount of unfavourable comment."[102] Although only Templar possessions of property could be seen in England, in places where the Templars had a strong military role opinions differed. In the Cyprus trials the Templars were known for their vigor in fighting with the Saracens and were held in high regard.[103] But, long before the trials, critics had emerged. William of Tyre, the chronicler of the Crusader States who played an important role in the politics of Jerusalem during Almaric's reign (1162-74), was a renowned Templar critic.[104] He claimed the Templars had lost their humility and had abandoned the patriarch of Jerusalem. Their tithes were no longer paid to the church, and they had

---

[102] Forey, *Military Orders*, 234.
[103] Ibid.
[104] Barber, *Trial of the Templars*, 16.

lost sight of their vocation to guard the pilgrims during their passage to the Holy Lands.[105]

In 1207, even Innocent III, who as pope was the order's theoretical overlord, wrote a letter to Philip of Plessis, the Master of the Templars, with complaints and concerns about Templar recruitment. Innocent III writes that the Templars "do not care about adding sin to sin like a long rope, alleging that, whoever having collected two or three denarii annually for them, will have joined their fraternity."[106] The Roman reformers were constantly fighting all forms of simony. The Templars went to severe lengths to eliminate simony. In fact, the first and foremost reason a brother could be kicked out of the Templars and lose his habit would be due to simony. The *Rule* states,

> The first thing for which a brother of the Temple may be expelled from the house is simony, for a brother who enters the house through simony should be expelled because of it; for he cannot save his soul. And simony is committed by gift or promise to a brother of the Temple or to another who may help him to enter into the Order of the Temple.[107]

Donations to the church were always accepted, but it was required that the Templars bequeath all property to the order upon joining. A Templar could not own property, but when he donated it to the Templars as he entered it might appear simoniacal. Also, issues arose when someone would leave his property to the Templars upon death, to

---

[105] "William of Tyre on the Templars," in Barber, *Trial of the Templars*, 16.
[106] "Pope Innocent III to Phillip of Plessis (1207)," in Barber, *Trial of the Templars*, 17. This particular citation pertains to simony.
[107] Upton-Ward, *French Rule,* 73.

ensure his soul's passage to heaven and to gain an ecclesiastical burial. This angered Pope Innocent III who claimed that the Order had recruited members who

> cannot lawfully be deprived of ecclesiastical burial, even if they are excommunicate; and through this, adulterers, manifest usurers and other false criminals excommunicated from the Church are, by insolence of this kind, buried in their cemeteries just like the Catholic faithful.[108]

In 1265, the Templars came under attack by another pope, Clement IV, who felt that his papal authority over the order was being ignored. Clement IV gives the Templars an eerie foreshadowing of the events to come when he reminds them that if at any point the Church

> removed for a short while the hand of its protection from you in the face of the prelates and the secular princes, you could not in any way subsist against the assaults of these prelates or the force of the princes.[109]

Regardless of the papal rebukes, and the inflamed letters, the popes as well as the princes knew that the Templars were necessary to maintain a presence in the Holy Land.

---

[108] Ibid. This situation pertains to the manipulation of ecclesiastical burials.

[109] "Pope Clement IV to the Grand Master of the Templars" (1265), in Barber, *Trial of the Templars*, 17.

Mission Failure

Unfortunately for the Templars, a new slave dynasty, known as the Mamlukes, had taken control of the Egyptian Sultanate.[110] They were brutal warriors, notorious for slaughtering all the inhabitants of a city or fortress upon claiming it. Acre was a heavily fortified city, with two layers of walls, and many towers strategically placed along them for defense. It was easily supplied by sea, as it had a strong natural harbor protected by the Templar citadel at its tip. Mamluke aggression had been anticipated after Al-Khalil had revoked the previous 10 year truce. As the siege of Acre began, the Templars, the Hospitallers and the Cypriots were at the walls in full force. Then the towers began to crumble, forcing the defenders to retreat to the inner walls. Under the guise of night, King Henry II of Cyprus, the Hospitallers, and their soldiers fled the city. The Templar grand master William of Beaujeu was killed in the following bloody onslaught as the Templars fought inside the streets of Acre, protecting the citizens who could not find passage out of the city.

For ten days the Templars were besieged in Acre at their headquarters. Despite the siege, the Templars had access to supplies through a port in their fortress. The commander, Theobald Gaudin, took advantage of this as he left the fortress the night of the 25th of May, with what could be transported of the Templar's eastern treasures and sailed to Sidon, an island fortress off the cost of the mainland.[111] Attempts to negotiate surrender were possibly for the many surviving Acre

---

[110] For more on the Mamlukes, see: Michael Winter and Amalia Levanoni, eds, *The Mamluks in Egyptian and Syrian Politics and Society* (Leiden: Brill, 2004).
[111] Barber, *New Knighthood*, 178.

47

inhabitants who had fled inside the headquarters.[112] With Gaudin and the ships gone, the Templars had no means to save them as they did not have had enough ships. Even in the end, their duty was to the pilgrims. Al-Khalil finally breached the walls, and the Templars fought to the last man as their fortress collapsed upon them. All left inside were massacred.[113] On the 28th of May, 1291, the Mamlukes took possession of the Templar stronghold in the city of Acre.[114]

With the fall of Acre, the Templars held only Atlit, Sidon, and Tortosa, all of which were abandoned within three months.[115] The last to be evacuated, Atlit, "had symbolized the Templar commitment to the Holy Land; it had never been taken by storm and thereafter the Mamluks dismantled it to ensure that it would never need to be."[116] The "Templar of Tyre", a chronicler of the Templars who had worked for the Order's secretariat in the east,[117] regrettably noted in retrospect, "This time, everything was lost, so that the Christians no longer held a palm of the land in Syria."[118] Without the Holy Land, the Templars had failed to accomplish what they had sworn under God to do, to defend the Holy Land. Their original vocation as defenders of pilgrims had become impossible because they had lost all mainland fortresses and cities. All that was left under their possession in the Holy Land was their estates on

---

[112] For more on the rescue of pilgrims by the Templars see M. Favreau-Lilie, "The Military Orders and the Escape of the Christian Population from the Holy Land in 1291," *The Journal of Medieval History,* 19 (1993): 201-227.
[113] Ibid.
[114] Ibid.
[115] Ibid.
[116] Ibid.
[117] Ibid., 167.
[118] Ibid., 178.

the island of Cyprus to which they were forced to retreat.[119] With the Holy Lands lost, the Knights Templar were now a large group of warrior monks, holding tremendous properties and wealth, and answerable only to the bishop of Rome, but lacking an immediate mission. The new grand master, James of Molay, tried to regain a foothold in the Holy Land. He engineered a siege of the island Ruad, which ended in complete disaster, as well an alliance with the Mongols which was disrupted by a Mongol civil war. A decade of squandered resources, and repeated failures in the Holy Lands, and the popular resentment against them would allow King Philip IV of France to systematically destroy what had taken centuries to build.

Friday the 13th

On the 24th of August 1307, Clement V responded to King Philip IV's concerns over the Knights Templar.[120] After an introduction filled with praise and adulation, Clement V begins to comment on the Templar situation which Philip IV had been repeatedly bringing to his attention, "inflamed with the zeal of the faith and devotion."[121] "Incredible and impossible" accusations were now causing Clement V to "harbour doubts", which caused "sorrow and turmoil in [his] heart."[122] Clement mentions that several rumors were reaching his ears, and that even the Master of the Knights of the Temple had already mentioned these rumors and had asked for absolution of the Templar name. In summation, Clement reminds Philip that his numerous remarks were not falling on

---

[119] Ibid., 183.

[120] For a biography of Clement V, see Sophia Menache, *Clement* (New York: Cambridge University Press, 1998).

[121] "Letter of Clement V to Philip IV (24 August 1307)," in Barber and Bate. *Templars: Selected Sources*, 243.

[122] Ibid.

deaf ears and that "at the insistence of the said Master and the Templars, and with the advice of our brothers, we propose to begin an enquiry of careful investigation of this matter."[123] Clement V also admonishes Philip in this letter that *he* will inform *him* about the Church's decision and what *they, the Church,* intend to do about the situation. The purpose of the letter seems to be to reassure Philip that the matter was being looked into, and that Clement is already well aware of the rumors that Philip brings to the table from his churchmen. Clement V is telling Philip that he needs to leave the Templars to be dealt with by the church. The Templars, since the papal bull of 1139, were an order of the church answerable only to the papacy, and not under the jurisdiction of a king.[124]

Despite the warning of Clement V to Philip IV that the matter was in the hands of the pope and not in those of the king, Philip issued warrants of arrest for the Templars on the 14th of September 1307.[125] These were secret warrants to be opened simultaneously. Philip begins his letter that he writes to the "faithful lord of Onival and John of Tourville" as "Philip, by the grace of God King of the Franks."[126] However, he had not yet received any direction or verdict from Pope Clement V since his last correspondence on the 24th of August. Philip writes to his nobles,

> there has recently echoed in our ears, to our not inconsiderable astonishment and vehement horror, vouched for by many people worthy to be believed, a bitter thing, a lamentable thing, a thing horrible to

---

[123] Ibid., 244.

[124] Marilyn Hopkins, *The Enigma of the Knights Templar: Their History and Mystical Connections* (St. Paul: Consortium Books, 2007), 25.

[125] "Philip IV's *Order for the Arrests*" (14 September 1307), in Barber and Bate, *Templars: Selected Sources*, 244.

[126] Ibid.

contemplate, terrible to hear, a heinous crime, and execrable evil, and abominable deed, a hateful disgrace, a completely inhuman thing, indeed remote from all humanity.[127]

Philip continues that the Templars have "forsaken God" and "made offerings to devils and not to God."[128] Philip goes into detail about these "lamentable things" in his arrest orders.[129] After calling the knights of the Order "wolves in sheep's clothing", Philip IV claims that he has received very reliable reports on the initiation rituals of the Order.[130] Upon entering the Order, Philip claims that the new member is confronted with an image of Christ's crucifixion in which he must look Christ in eyes, deny him three times, and then spit in his face three times.[131] He is then forced to remove his clothes of the secular world, and naked in the presence of the leader of the house, receive a kiss from the leader on the lower back, the navel, and then on the mouth.[132] Philip IV then proceeds to claim that being a member of the order "bounds one to accept the request of another to perform the vice of that horrible, dreadful intercourse, and this is why the wrath of God has fallen on these sons of infidelity."[133]

---

[127] Ibid.

[128] Ibid., 245.

[129] For a view of Philip's insincerity, see: Sylvia Schein, "Philip IV the Fair and the Crusade: A Reconsideration," in *Crusade and Settlement: Papers Read at the First Conference of the Society for the Study of the Crusades and the Latin East and Presented to R.C. Smail*, ed. Peter W. Edbury (Atlantic Highlands: Humanities Press, 1985).

[130] "Philip IV's *Order for the Arrests*" (14 September 1307), in Barber and Bate, *Templars: Selected Sources*, 245.

[131] Ibid.

[132] Ibid.

[133] Ibid.

Philip's final claim is that the brothers have given up the "source of living water" and have exchanged it for the "Calf" and made offerings to idols.[134] These allegations are backed up by what Philip IV claims to be "a full investigation to determine the truth in these matters" and "a numerous increase in the number of informers."[135] Further, Philip claims that after meeting with "the most holy father in the Lord" Clement V, that he has been "placed by the Lord on the watchtower of regal eminence to defend the liberty of the faith of the church."[136] Once again, Philip has claimed to be the white knight of the Roman Church, but in reality he has been given no authority to act by Clement. He claims that his authority is directly from the Lord. Philip placed at the head of this investigation the papal inquisitors, who were established by the papacy "but in France, controlled by the monarchy."[137] In fact, Philip claims that William of Paris, papal inquisitor, had "invoked the help of our arm" in dealing with these renegade knights.[138] Even though William of Paris was theoretically a deputy of the pope, he was closer to the king than to Clement.[139] William was not only a French Dominican, but at the time he held the position of royal confessor, and the king had frequently used his "inquisitor" as a strong arm of state power.[140]

To maintain secrecy, Philip ordered a discretionary investigation of all the religious houses under the pretense of verifying tithes.[141] First,

---

[134] Ibid.
[135] Ibid., 246.
[136] Ibid.
[137] Barber, *Trial of the Templars*, 57.
[138] Ibid., 60.
[139] Ibid., 61.
[140] Ibid.
[141] "Philip IV's *Order for the Arrests*" (14 September 1307), in Barber and Bate, *Templars: Selected Sources*, 247.

Philip concurs that although not all may be guilty of said crimes, all must be arrested and "tested in the furnace like gold and cleared by the due process of judicial examination."[142] This ensures that all potential enemies would be in the custody of the king, and that he would be able to release and determine innocence as he sees fit. Even those that were innocent in many cases would have given in due to the torture and folded early or they would have been so mutilated by this torture that they would be scarred for life.[143] Philip continues stating that "all individuals of the Order without exception within our kingdom shall be arrested and movable and immovable goods shall be seized, and these seizures kept in good faith in our possession."[144] The royal legates selected to execute the arrests were to be chosen by the local nobility, but Philip recommended choosing "powerful *prud'hommes*" that were "above suspicion."[145] To protect all property seized, Philip recommended also that competent farmers and custodians should "ensure that the vines and estates are cultivated and planted properly."[146]

Trials and Confessions

Upon hearing of Philip IV's arrest of the Templars earlier in the month, Pope Clement V was furious at his audacity. In contrast to the noble and respectful beginning of his August 24th letter, where Clement V called Philip the illustrious king of the Franks and offered his apostolic

---

[142] Ibid., 246.

[143] Piers Paul Read, *The Templars* (New York: St. Martin's Press, 1999), 279.

[144] "Philip IV's *Order for the Arrests*" (14 September 1307), in Barber and Bate, *Templars: Selected Sources,* 246.

[145] Ibid.

[146] Ibid.

blessing, here he begins this letter with "Dearest Son."[147] Clement recalls how Philip's ancestors,

> recognized that all things pertaining to the Christian faith lay in the jurisdiction of the Roman See for which they maintained their respect even to this day... the ship of Peter was buffeted by many dangers ... they nevertheless decided in many varied published pronouncements that in matters concerning religion and especially in those in which the ecclesiastical and religious persons could be harmed, they would not reserve anything for their own courts of justice, but would leave everything to the ecclesiastical courts, acknowledging that in aforesaid cases and persons nothing remained for them except obedience to the Apostolic See when it was asked of them.[148]

Clement had asked Philip for obedience and for patience. He is apparently infuriated that Philip would take the matter of the Templars to his own courts without respecting the jurisdiction of the pope.

Clement might have recognized the true motives of Philip when he stated that he was aware that "you have laid hands upon the persons and the *goods* of the Templars."[149] These goods of which Clement spoke were the property of the Church, since the Templars were merely a warrior hand of the Pope, and Clement was reminding Philip that this property is that of the Church and not spoils of war to be given to his nobles. Although at this point the situation seemed in the hands of Philip IV, and not of Clement, he stated that he had already alerted his cardinals, Beranger and Stephen, to remind Philip that this is in the papacy's

---

[147] "Letter of Clement V to Philip IV" (27 October 1307), in Barber and Bate, *Templars: Selected Sources*, 249.
[148] Ibid.
[149] Ibid.

hands.[150] To augment this point, Clement also showed fear that the Templar property may not be returned to him, and wrote

> there is no room for us to doubt that very quickly, today rather than tomorrow, if there were present those who could receive in our name the persons and goods from your hand, you would acquiesce and hand them over into our possession, to this end, in order to expedite matters in all security and with due respect, we are intending to send to your Highness the aforementioned cardinals [Stephen and Beranger].[151]

Clement V expects all the property taken by the king to be transferred to cardinals, not to the French nobles or the royal treasury. Clement also takes time to mention that these men of the Church were not only held as prisoners, but had suffered more than just imprisonment.[152] These actions, Clement argues, are a direct "insult to and contempt of our person together with that of the Roman Church."[153] It is also important at this time to reiterate that Clement V still is uncertain that there is an "infection" and if so, "God forbid!"[154] In Poitiers in 1308, Clement V in refuting Philip's claim that he had papal authority for the arrests, proclaimed that the "procedure for the arrest of the Templars was never sanctioned by his letters."[155]

---

[150] Ibid., 250.

[151] Ibid.

[152] Ibid.

[153] "Letter of Clement V to Philip IV" (27 October 1307), in Barber and Bate. *Templars: Selected Sources*, 250.

[154] Ibid.

[155] Barber, *The Trial of the Templars*, 62.

The Chinon Parchment is a lost relic related to the fate of the Templars, a rediscovered papal absolution that was never enacted.[156] The importance of this is that Pope Clement V on August 17th, 1308, absolved in the document Grand Master James of Molay of the Templars, and the many other heads of the order who were currently under arrest.[157] This absolution gave these Templars a chance to be reinstated into the Catholic communion, and to be readmitted to receive the sacraments.[158] This absolution appeared while the first phase of the French inquisitor's trial was occurring. Clement V, pursuing his original intentions to maintain the jurisdiction over the Templars and to decide their fate, enacted his own absolution, regardless of the current status of Philip IV's investigation. The Chinon Parchment reads

> Having acted according to the mandate and commissioned by the said Lord Supreme Pontif [Clement V], we questioned the aforementioned grandmaster [James of Molay] and the preceptors and examined them concerning the matters described above. Their words and confessions were written down exactly the way they are included here by the notaries whose names are listed below in the presence of witnesses listed below. We also ordered these things drawn up in this official form and validated by the protection of our seals.[159]

The "official" papal legates, those sent by Clement V himself, in doing their own personal interrogations had discovered evidence quite different than that secured by the French government. Specifically, the

---

[156] Frale, "The Chinon Chart," 109-134.
[157] Ibid.
[158] Ibid.
[159] "The Chinon Parchment: Were the Knights Templar Pardoned ?" *In Rebus*. 2007. http://www.inrebus.com/chinon.php (accessed April 5, 2010).

Grand Master James of Molay, whom the French had tortured into making a full confession, had another confession to tell the pontiff's men.

> Concerning the way of his initiation into the Order, he said that having given him the cloak the receptor showed to him <the cross> and told him that he should denounce the God whose image was depicted on that cross, and that he should spit on the cross. Which he did, although he did not spit on the cross, but near it, according to his words. He also said that he performed this denunciation in words, not in spirit. Regarding the sin of sodomy, the worshipped head and the practice of illicit kisses, he, diligently questioned, said that he knew nothing of that.[160]

Clement V felt that his own investigation was complete, and was ready to readmit the Templars not only into the Church but perhaps also into a reformed Order, possibly merged with the other military orders.[161]

> We concluded to extend the mercy of absolution for these acts to brother Jaques de Molay, the grandmaster of the said order, who in the form and manner described above had denounced in our presence the described and any other heresy, and swore in person on the Lord's Holy Gospel, and humbly asked for the mercy of absolution, restoring him to unity with the Church and reinstating him to communion of the faithful and sacraments of the Church.[162]

Mounting pressure from Philip led Clement to abandon the solution set forth in the Parchment of Chinon in favor of a papal commission to hear the trial itself, to be held in his presence in Paris. The

---

[160] Ibid.

[161] Frale, "The Chinon Chart," 109-134.

[162] "The Chinon Parchment: Were the Knights Templar Pardoned ?" *In Rebus.* 2007. http://www.inrebus.com/chinon.php (accessed April 5, 2010).

Templars who had volunteered to defend the Order in the trial in Paris were handed 127 charges of which they were being accused.[163] Peter of Bologna, and Reginald of Provins, Templar knights with a notable service record in the Holy Land, appeared in front of the papal commission to testify and because they had never confessed to any charges of heresy, they could not be charged as relapsed heretics.[164] Reginald claimed that the brothers of the Order had been led through the hearings at present as if "sheep to the slaughter", and their confessions had been extracted by "diverse and various kinds of tortures, from which many had died, many were forever disabled, and many at that time driven to lie against themselves and the Order."[165] Reginald argued to the papal commission that "torture removed any freedom of mind, which is what every good man ought to have."[166] He even claimed that the brothers within the Order were bribed with lifetime pensions by the king if they merely confessed, and that the situation of the Order was already solved and condemned.[167] Reginald and Peter's excellent defense of the order, specifically in their efforts in showing the nobility of the members within the order, and their strong upbringing which could not possibly have allowed such heresy, led the pontiff to recess the papal commission and postpone the final judgment due to endless deliberations.[168]

To handle this new defense of the Templars, Philip IV "reacted by initiating a real blackmail mechanism."[169] The "royally" placed Archbishop of Sens, Philip of Marigny, indebted to King Philip IV,

---

[163] Read, *The Templars,* 278.
[164] Ibid., 279.
[165] Ibid.
[166] Ibid.
[167] Ibid., 280.
[168] Ibid.
[169] Barber, *Trial of the Templars,* 175.

reinitiated his individual inquiries against members of the Order within his province and swiftly tried the 54 Templars.[170] Before the pope or any other authority besides the king could react, due to the papal commission's current status of recess, the archbishop began his attack.[171] On May 12, 1310 the 54 Templars, having been previously transferred to secular authorities by the archbishop, were burnt at the stake, the death of a heretic.[172] The two Templar defenders who had led the defense, Peter and Reginald, now also faced the wrath of Philip IV. Peter "mysteriously disappeared" and Reginald was sentenced to perpetual imprisonment.[173] With the removal of the Templar's heroes and the horrific execution of the 54 in Sens, the Templar defense was "effectively silenced."[174]

The trial against the Templars culminated in the council of Vienne, in which Philip IV forced Pope Clement V to make a final judgment on the Templars. Clement's advisors earlier during the trials at Vienne could not decide on whether to give the Templars another hearing or suppress the order immediately.[175] Clement even spoke on the 20th of March 1312, that he was unsure whether the Order of the Temple should be conserved or destroyed.[176] Unfortunately for Clement, Philip's final assault on the Templars was at hand.[177] The same day Pope Clement V professed uncertainty, King Philip IV of France, along with his brothers Charles and Louis and his three sons, arrived at the Council in Vienne to

---

[170] Ibid., 3.
[171] Read. *Templars,* 280.
[172] Barber, *Trial of the Templars*, 3.
[173] Ibid.
[174] Ibid.
[175] Barber, *Trial of the Templars*, 267.
[176] Ibid.
[177] Frale, "The Chinon Chart," 109-134.

greet Clement, and assist him in his judgment, with an entire army.[178] Philip had solved a "disagreement" with Boniface VIII years earlier by sending William Nogaret to Anagni with a military force, and he appears have dealt with Clement in similar fashion. Clement V would no longer protest against the will of Philip, knowing too well the potentially fatal wrath of Philip. Within two days, he solved the issue at hand.

Vox in excelso, the papal bull suppressing the Knights Templar, was then read aloud to the council with Philip present.

> Considering therefore the infamy, suspicion, noisy insinuation and the other things above which have been brought against the Order, and also the secret and clandestine reception of the brothers of this Order … considering, moreover, the grave scandal which has arisen from these things against the Order, which it did not seem could be checked while this Order remained in being, and also the danger both to faith and souls, and that many horrible things have been done by very many of the brothers of this Order, who have lapsed into the sin of wicked apostasy … the crime of detestable idolatry, and the execrable outrage of the Sodomites . . . not without bitterness and sadness of heart … we abolish the aforesaid Order of the Temple, and its constitution, habit and name by an irrevocable and perpetually valid decree; and we subject it to perpetual prohibition with the approval of the Holy Council, strictly forbidding anyone to presume to enter the said Order in the future, or to receive or wear its habit, or to act as a Templar.[179]

Clement V thus concluded the Templar trial, and suppressed the Order permanently. He stipulated that any other investigation or

---

[178] Barber, *Trial of the Templars*, 267.
[179] "Vox in excelso," in Barber, *Trial of the Templars*, 268.

interference into the matter of the Templars would be "vexatious and worthless."[180]

Vox in excelso was augmented by the papal bull Ad providam, which handed over all Templar property to the Hospitallers.[181] King Philip IV was able to extract a large sum, 260,000 livres tournois, in order to repay the royal treasury for the substantial cost of the Templar trials and the safeguarding of the Templar property.[182] As Clement V had condemned the Order without giving his monastic warriors a hearing in Vienne, and Philip IV had finally suppressed the Templars, the Order was terminated. Philip's aggression had triumphed.

In other countries where trials were conducted without torture, most Templars had not been punished but their reputations were tarnished. Many former Templars joined monasteries or lived life beyond the spotlight, and eventually Vox in excelso solved any remaining disputes in the courts. Philip's triumph resulted in the global destruction of the Templars, leaving a power vacuum in military and financial systems throughout the world to be filled by the nobility and the emerging Italian bankers. The torture-induced confessions, however incriminating, were unique to France. Elsewhere, confessions were not obtained until after torture was introduced, and still were quite rare. In retrospect, the verdicts of the trials outside of France were overshadowed due to the universality of Clement's suppression of the Templars. Regardless of their guilt or innocence, regardless of Philip's motive, the die had been cast on October 13th, and there was no place left for this relic of the crusades to remain. With their vocation and sworn oath to protect

---

[180] Ibid.
[181] Ibid., 271.
[182] Ibid., 272.

the pilgrimage lost, and their respect and pride throughout Europe tainted, so too were they.

Chapter V

Were the Templars Guilty as Charged?

… they declare that if the brothers of the Temple have said , say now or in the future during their captivity anything against themselves and the Order of the Temple, this should not harm the said Order, since it is obvious that they will have spoken or will speak under compulsion, force or corruption, persuasion, bribery or from fear.

–Templars Peter of Bologna and Reginald of Provins[183]

The many sins and crimes charged against the Knights Templar are now in retrospect less clear than Philip IV had proclaimed. The Templars were held by the French crown for nearly seven years, giving the inquisitors plenty of time to extract the "truth" by the means of torture.[184] Although the confessions obtained by the French inquisitors were numerous, in Iberia, England, Scotland, and other Templar areas, their confessions were either completely absent or very few.[185] In Cyprus, Aragon, and England where torture was not used, the inquisitors were not able to document any confessions until the summer of 1311, when in

---

[183] "Defence of the Order by a group of Templars" (7 April 1310), in Barber and Bate. *Templars: Selected Sources*, 298.
[184] Anne Gilmour-Bryson, "Italian Templar Trials: Truth or Falsehood," in *Knighthoods of Christ: Essays on the History of the Crusades and the Knights Templar Presented to Malcolm Barber*, ed. Norman Housley (Burlington: Ashgate, 2007), 209.
[185] Ibid.

England torture was implemented.[186] In fact, the confessions which were obtained in France differed in each location at which they were obtained, included many conflicting facts, and presented different reasons behind the initiation ritual which was allegedly so heretical.[187] Although Philip insisted on the accuracy of the confessions which he had obtained in his inquisition against the Templars, these confessions may not be as credible as they once seemed.

Despite the many reconstructions by scholars of the guilt of the Templars and the motives of Philip IV, I feel that another is necessary to continue strides made by Barbara Frale, but in relation to more than just the denial of Christ. When taking into account the absolution and trial documents mentioned by Frale, and then comparing them to new understandings about the Templar *Rule* and its purpose in initiation, a reconstruction which better relates the history of the Templars and their trial seems possible. If each major accusation is analyzed in regards to *Rule*, tradition, and what is known of the initiation rite, the background of the charges becomes clearer.

Idol worship and Absolution of Sins

The complete lack of idols found on which the supposed "idolatry" took place would lead some to find the Templars completely innocent of this charge, but more investigation is needed. Of course the many Templars outside of France would have had time to destroy or hide any such idols, but the swiftness and secretive nature of the attacks on Friday the 13th which Philip IV had carefully planned would not have

---

[186] Barber, *Trial of the Templars*, 283.
[187] Forey, *Military Orders*, 232.

allowed for this.[188] The Templars were taken in France with such surprise that few were able to resist, and most were unarmed upon arrest, where in Aragon half a dozen Templar strongholds were besieged in order to capture the members of the Order.[189] As the French chapter houses were searched and inventoried, a complete absence of incriminating evidence is noticeable, no Baphomets or calf heads were found.[190] Regardless of whether or not there had been opportunities to destroy the idols, if these had in fact existed, some of the tortured Templars ought to have described them in similar fashion.

The Templars were known for their devotion to relics as well as their collection of them. This is not a question of the more renowned relics such as the Holy Grail, the Shroud of Turin, and the Ark of the Covenant that have been linked to them through fiction and legend, rather there is evidence for their connection with other relics, such as that of the True Cross. However, it is not reverence of relics which gets the Templars scrutiny; it is the alleged idols. Most importantly, despite exhausting itemization and inspection of the Templar houses, in France and throughout Europe, there is never any surfacing of any Mahomet or cat idols. However, the "head" could very easily have been a misunderstood representation of heads of saints, and other relics which the Templars did possess. In fact, the most notorious of these was the head of St. Euphemia. Brother John of Villa, draper of the Order, mentioned when accused of idolatry that, "he never knew, nor knows that such heads of idols or idols were in the order. He said nevertheless, that

---

[188] Ibid., 231.
[189] Ibid., 226.
[190] Ibid., 231.

the head of St Euphemia is in the order."[191] Therefore, the idea that there were heads does create an opportunity which could be misinterpreted or purposely misunderstood.

Abuses involving the absolution of sins are known in Christian tradition. Peter Damian feared that two priests could connive to absolve each other. Or absolution could be granted by someone who did not have the ecclesiastical right to do so. The Templars had been accused of in-house absolution of sins, either by the master or by the head of the commandery. Also, there was the controversial claim that the Templars had been forced to confess only to their chaplain brothers, and were forbidden to confess to anyone outside of the Order. Although there is some merit in the argument that they were told to confess to chaplain brothers first, the claim that the Templar master absolved brothers seems to be another misinterpretation. Evelyn Lord has argued in her book *The Knights Templar in Britain* that regular members had confused the sacrament of absolution in the Catholic tradition with the absolution of members in regards to breakings of the Templar *Rule* which the master did have authority to give.[192] The *Rule* itself states that the Templars were punished by the master and the chapter for failing the *Rule* and habit, so it can be assumed that the master and the chapter could forgive these sins as well. In fact, there is a whole section in the French *Rule* on the things which a chaplain brother can absolve and on "the things which a chaplain brother may not absolve."[193] There is even evidence of times where, in the case of simony, the chaplain brother was forbidden to absolve the

---

[191] Anne Gilmour-Bryson, *The Trial of the Templars in Cyprus* (Boston: Brill, 1998), 140.
[192] Evelyn Lord. *The Knights Templar in Britain* (London: Longman, 2002), 196.
[193] Upton-Ward, *French Rule*, 80.

brother, and the case was sent to the archbishop.[194] The Catalan *Rule* of the Templars is more incriminating. The *Rule* itself claims that,

> The chaplain brothers should hear the confessions of the brothers, and no brother should make confession to anyone else but him, since he may see the chaplain brother without permission; for he has a greater power to absolve them on behalf of the Pope than a bishop... If a chaplain brother sins, he should plead for mercy like any other brother, without kneeling in chapter, and should do what the brothers sentence him to do.[195]

A servant or sergeant brother, who was not well versed in the theological language of sacrament and absolution, could easily have confused the master or the chapter absolving his secular sins against the habit in regards to Templar issues with the absolutions of spiritual sins which would need a priest to absolve. For crimes of spirit, the Templar chaplain did have authority to absolve these as he was an authorized priest of the Catholic Church. The papal bull *Omne datum optimum* in 1139 confirms this. However, it does seem likely that some sins by Templars may have been absolved in chapter, especially those of the chaplain brothers. If this was in fact the case, their *Rule* itself incriminates them of this and anyone who could get his hands on the *Rule* would see this error.

Brother Stephen the Spaniard, of Portugal, Knight of the Temple, made an interesting point in his deposition in Cyprus. Although he denied that Templars were forbidden to confess to priests outside the Templars, if a Templar chaplain was available, "they were forbidden to

---

[194] Upton-Ward, *Catalan Rule*, 51.
[195] Ibid., 25.

67

confess to others."[196] Although it sounds incriminating, this seems like it is just an attempt to keep Templar business within the house, and if it is not necessary to confess outside the Temple, then one need not do so. Regardless, if a chaplain was not available, then they were allowed to confess outside the Order, showing clearly that the Templars were in no way impeding reconciliation, but they were creating rules which, after being found in the Catalan *Rule*, could easily bring suspicion on themselves.

Closed Reception and Secrecy of Ceremony

Entry into a Templar commandery--which could in some cases be an armed fortress, tower or chapel--could be intimidating and difficult. One of the major concerns and allegations against the Templars was that the initiation ceremony was secret or held at night and that no one was allowed in except members of the Order. It was and still is common for monastic orders to hold their chapter meetings in private. In the trial records in Cyprus, Brother Hubert of the diocese of Vienne, full knight of the order of the Temple, tried to make it clear to his inquisitor that the initiation ritual occurred during chapter meetings which only members of the order could attend. He also reminded them that no one who was not a member would be allowed to enter. He specifically states that guards were always placed outside the door during chapter meetings, especially chapter meetings in which reception occurred.[197] This is reinforced by the Templar grand marshal, Ayme of Osseliers' deposition. Also in Cyprus, he was the first to be interrogated of the Templars. He stated that reception occurred "in the order openly in the presence of brothers of the

---

[196] Gilmour-Bryson, *Trial of the Templars in Cyprus,* 186.
[197] Ibid., 163.

order, not of others."[198] He reinforced this by saying that "brothers indeed used to put guards on the doors of the house when they had a chapter meeting so that no one, who was not of the chapter, could approach without permission."[199] During reception specifically, Ayme stated, "brothers indeed put guards on the doors of the house when they held a chapter meeting when a brother is received into the order, and no one who was not of the chapter, could then have access to them."[200]

Ayme, Grand Marshal of the Templars, without torture or persuasion, clearly admitted that the chapters were held in secret, barring all non-members for the receptions. In fact, the new initiates are clearly detained as they are unreachable by outsiders. Yet, Ayme does not seem to see anything unusual about this. In fact many modern fraternal, social, and monastic institutions conduct closed door meetings to discuss private business and are not considered in any way illicit.

Secrecy was required for Templar initiation because what was spoken during initiation about the failures of house and habit was very incriminating. The Templars ultimately were suppressed because at the trial their reputation was damaged. If the outside community had heard of tales of Templars who had apostatized, or who had carnal relations with a brother, that reputation might have been tarnished earlier. These were the very stories told during reception, according to the Templar *Rule*, and it could very well have been these exact stories which became their undoing when they reached the ear of Philip.

---

[198] Ibid., 157.
[199] Ibid., 159.
[200] Ibid.

Illicit Kisses and Homosexuality

The illicit kisses of which the Templars were accused appear to be a misunderstanding of the monastic tradition of the kiss of peace. In regards to the kisses that occurred during reception, Ayme of Osseliers added that the Templars actually, "made the man being received kiss the cross with reverence, and he subsequently kissed the receiver and the priest-chaplain ... on the mouth."[201] The kiss, which was commonly bestowed on neophytes in ordination and baptism, was not illicit in nature, and is similar to the kiss of peace. In many cases, this practice continues today in modern monastic initiations, such as that of the Order of Saint Benedict, where the initiate exchanges the kiss of peace with each brother, asking for his prayers. [202] Brother Nicholas of Peccia was an Englishman from Ardena, who was the fifth Templar interrogated in Cyprus. He went into more detail about the kissing of the chaplain by stating that the kiss was "on the mouth as a sign of peace and concord."[203] In Cyprus, where no torture occurred, all the Templars freely admitted to the kiss of peace at reception. To them, it was nothing to be ashamed of, but to a secular knight not knowledgeable about monastic tradition such things might be misunderstood. Where torture may have occurred in the Patrimony of Saint Peter, Guillelmus of Verduno stated that he had received the ritual kiss at his reception on the mouth, and that he knew nothing of illicit kisses.[204]

---

[201] Gilmour-Bryson, *Trial of the Templars in Cyprus,* 156.

[202] Kardong, *Benedict,* 476.

[203] Gilmour-Bryson, *Trial of the Templars in Cyprus,* 172.

[204] Anne Gilmour-Bryson, *The Trial of Templars in the Papal State and the Abruzzi* (Città del Vaticano: Biblioteca Apostolica Vaticana, 1982), 41.

Homosexuality is another case entirely. The accusation that homosexuality was practiced within the Order is almost certainly true. The *Rule* itself mentions situations where it had occurred and strict punishments were made. The Catalan *Rule* tells of a Templar horror story where,

> It happened at Chateau Pelerin that there were brothers who practiced wicked sin and caressed each other at night, so that those close to the evil deed and others who had suffered by it, told this thing to the Master and to a group of worthy men. The Master took the advice that this thing should not come to chapter because the deed was so offensive, and that the brothers should be made to come to Acre. And when they had arrived, the Master sent a worthy man to the chamber where they had been placed, and made them remove their habits and put them in heavy irons.[205]

Therefore, clearly Templar homosexuality, although heavily condemned, was admitted by official Templar documents to have had occurred in the past. Once again, anyone outside of the Templars who could hear these rumors would be quite shocked.

Within monastic houses homosexuality was always at least potential problem. Illicit acts occurring between brothers of the Temple were not unique to this religious order. It was a constant issue in monastic institutions, and is indeed in all human communities, past and present. Regardless, what is at issue is whether the Templars actively encouraged illicit carnal relations between brothers during reception. Continuing from the rumors of the illicit kisses, the logical next stage of accusation would be to imply that carnal relations were also forced. Almost universally, the brothers who were interrogated denied that they were involved with any

---

[205] Upton-Ward, *Catalan Rule*, 71.

71

illicit homosexual activity. However, some mentioned that they had heard of it, and others mentioned that it was encouraged at reception. In Cyprus Ayme of Osselier said that it was not true, and his brothers in Cyprus unanimously agreed with him.

It seems that there was at least at one time a scandal in the Templars where certain brothers were accused of homosexuality but were quickly punished. After this, the tale of the punishment was placed inside the *Rule* as a warning of the consequences of such actions; just as many other failures of house and habit were also put into the *Rule*. Therefore, cases of homosexuality were discussed in the initiation ritual but apparently in order to condemn them and warn against them. This mentioning of illicit carnal actions within the *Rule* just during the initiation ritual, coupled with a licit kiss on the mouth at reception, could have possibly laid the foundation for the accusations of homosexuality within the Order at the trials.

Defamation of Christ and Cross

There have been many attempts to explain how knights devoted to protecting Christ's Holy Land could have denied him during initiation. Remembering the failures of the apostle Peter when he denied Christ in the gospels could have been the source for the Templars to mention the story. Others have attributed the denials and spitting on the cross to the horrible experiences of a founding father of the Order who was captured by Saracens during the first crusade.[206] What is agreed on by the sources is that there was a cross at the reception ceremony. In fact, crucifixes were present in all chapels in this era. Every major Templar commandery

---

[206] Forey, *Military Orders*, 233.

had a chapel, in which the Templars would spend their daily matins and prime.[207] Ayme of Osseliers is recorded as responding in regards to the accusation of the spitting on the cross that, "he denies the contents of it to be true. On the contrary, he said that he, and others of the order, when he received someone into the order, made the man being received kiss the cross with reverence, and he subsequently kissed the receiver and the priest-chaplain then present, on the mouth."[208] This is interesting on many levels. First we notice that not only is the cross present, but it is presented to the initiate as they are "made" to kiss it with reverence. Also it gives us a time placement of the occurrence of the cross incident, placing it right before the kiss of peace.

One striking example is of a Brother named Roger Alaman, who was captured after the disastrous battle of La Forbie in 1244. After being captured by the Ayyubids, he was forced to recant Christianity and made to swear allegiance to Islam. No details were given of how in fact, whether through torture or fear of death, that the conversion was forced upon poor Roger. However, after being released from Ayyubid captivity, he was shamed and expelled from the Order once he told his master what had happened.[209] Some scholars, such as Barbara Frale have suggested that this forced recanting of the faith was then shown and enacted on the new initiate. The horrors of the act, which could have involved spitting or urinating on the cross and denouncing Christ, were similar to Muslims urinating on the True Cross after its capture at Hattin, or to it being dragged through the streets of Jerusalem.[210] Many pilgrims and crusaders

---

[207] Upton-Ward, *French Rule,* 82-83.
[208] Gilmour-Bryson, *Trial of the Templars in Cyprus,* 156.
[209] Upton-Ward, *Catalan Rule,* 71.
[210] For a similar example of Muslims marking the cross with urine in the Spanish theater, see "The Conquest of Lisbon: De expugnatione

had renounced the faith in order to live after capture. Templars were never to be captured, and a knight of Christ should never renounce Christ to a Muslim. Perhaps the initiate was shown this example, or in some cases physically forced to reenact it, in order to remind him to do what the Templars were made to do, to fight to the death, maintain the banner, and protect the Holy Land at pain of death. There was no surrender. This mentality is what gave the Templars their prowess on the battlefield. They were knights of Christ, and, because they had no fear of death, enemies knew that they were not to be taken lightly.

In "The Chinon Chart: Papal Absolution to the Last Templar, Master Jacques de Molay," Barbra Frale brings to light some evidence concerning the Templar's heretical charges, transcriptions from Clement's inquisitors who questioned the imprisoned Templars. These interviews were done secretly outside of the influence of Philip IV, and by papal inquisitors who were appointed by Clement. Frale has found that during the initiation ceremony of new Templars to the order, the Templars confessed that they acted a pretend scene in which they replicated an historic encounter in which a Templar was captured in the Holy Land by a Saracen.[211] Frale concluded from her evidence that "The Templars admitted that during the entrance ceremony they had denied Jesus Christ and spat on the Cross, but repeated again and again before the pontiff that they were threatened with prison or even death anyway,

---

Lyxbonensi," trans. Charles Wendell David, Records of Civilization, Sources and Studies, 24 (New York: Columbia University Press, 2001), 133.
[211] Ibid., 126.

74

they never consented to this in their soul, and as soon as possible, they confessed to a priest and asked for absolution."[212]

Frale seems to argue that what may have been simple initiation rituals of the neophytes to the Templars, enacted to show what would happen if they were captured in the Holy Land, were manipulated to show the Templars as heretics deserving death. Although the initiation rituals may have been simply acting, Frale acknowledges that Clement felt that the Templars "were surely so tainted by bad habits that they needed reform, but they could not be considered as heretics."[213] On their guilt, Frale continues upon her analysis of the notes within the margin while the transcripts of the trial were taken, and probably written by Clement himself while reviewing these notes,

> "analyzing how the marginal notes were developed, and comparing them to all the other Templar confessions in the trial, classified by subject in a special electronic archive, it is possible to sketch out what Clement V and his advisors had probably understood: the strange profession ceremony was simply an entrance ritual, a custom which was common (with variation) in every military group since early antiquity. As a ritual of passage, it was a kind of secret appendix after the formal ceremony of profession which is described in the constitution as a compulsory test to which all men of the Temple had to submit, a peculiar tradition which had to show to the new brother the violence the Templars suffered when they were captured by Saracens, that is to say, they would be compelled to deny Christ and to spit on the cross."[214]

---

[212] Ibid.
[213] Ibid., 127.
[214] Ibid.

Frale further analyzes the ritual and offers the reader its purpose, "the main aim of the test was to strengthen the soul of recruits."[215] Whether this form of hazing occurred to many of the knights in France, who under extreme torture and prolonged imprisonment under Philip the Fair confessed to doing so, or whether it was the telling of poor Roger's story and legend which caught Philip's ear, enabling him to conjure up tales of heresy, would at this point be pure speculation. The trial documents as well as the Chinon Parchment both claim that the Templars would go through this and would then immediately confess with the Templar's chapter priest, or another. But other trial records deny this. One might speculate that given the popular tradition that monastic profession absolved all sin, a neophyte who was shaken by this frightening ritual would still at the end of the ceremony be able to see himself as justified, but would know that what he was capable of and that he would not find any similar lenience should he falter in his loyalty to Christ and the Order.

---

[215] Ibid.

Chapter VI

Conclusion

> We are silent here as to detail because the
> memory is so sad and unclean. With the approval of
> the sacred council we abolished the constitution of the
> Order, its habit and name, not without bitterness of
> heart.

–Papal Bull *Ad providam*[216]

The shocking fall of the Templars has prompted questions of motive, guilt, and conspiracy. It is simply too easy to ignore the bigger picture and just claim that Philip was greedy or that the Templars were heinous blasphemers. Despite centuries of defamation, and rehabilitation, the Templars are still controversial, even today viewed by some as noble righteous martyrs and by others as heretical gnostics. In reality, it seems that the Templars were merely a brotherhood of warrior-monks, who were attempting to unite their dual identities in very human ways. The focus on the greed of the Templars as financiers seems to be overstated by historians, inasmuch as their *Rule*--Primitive, French, and Catalan-- says nothing about the financial business, which should be surprising to

---

[216] "Papal Bull, Ad providam" (2 May 1312), in Barber and Bate. *Templars: Selected Sources*, 319.

those who see how much detail the *Rule* gives to every other aspect of Templar life.

The historiography seems to have shifted to people who feel that the Templars truly were guilty, in some shape or form. Frale suggests that the Templars had hazing rituals, which may have had some heretical aspects, although they were meant to warn the new Templars about the treacheries of the east. Riley-Smith has argued that there were perhaps heresies on the peripheries, or in small form, for which the entire brotherhood had to pay. Others, like Barber, just proclaim their innocence. Perhaps a closer look at the charges is necessary. The entire history of failures of house and habit had been written directly into the *Rule,* and these failures parallel every sin that Philip had charged against the Templars. Since it is known that the Templars read the rule to the initiate to their upmost capacity, it is very plausible that some physical hazing occurred to illustrate the failures, as Frale suggests. However, an outsider merely reading the *Rule* out of context might judge the Templars harshly. Carlo Ginzburg's *The Cheese and the Worms* is a prime example of how people can interpret texts in their own way.

In conclusion, what we know of the Templar initiation ceremony is pretty thorough. The wear and tear on the reception sections of the surviving *Rule* books, and the specific lines and quotations, such as "he

78

shall say" or direct lines which are intended to be read precisely by the Master, make it quite clear that the Rule was read and followed during reception. The only moment at which improvisation could occur, is in the secret room, where the two or three senior members are alone, with the initiate, preparing him during the chapter meeting. If it was at this time that some severe hazing occurred, or if it was after the reception when the master left and the new brother was at the mercy of his senior brothers, the sources differ. The confessions found in trial documents were taken under severe torture. In places such as Cyprus where the Templars were not tortured, there was not one single confession by a Templar of any sort of heresy or hazing during initiation. Yet initiation rituals may have been powerful. I would make the argument that this was necessary due to the fact that the probation period had been dropped and the "testing of the spirit" had to be accomplished in a much shorter period of time.

Although the Templars were monks following a monastic rule, they were also battle hardened warriors, many who had watched with their own eyes their brothers slain and sacrificed on the field of war. And those returning after disasters such as Hattin or La Forbie, despite new lax recruitment regulations, may still have wanted to ensure that their brothers were "battle ready". A Templar knight who had experienced firsthand during his reception the horrors of being captured by the

79

Saracens would know exactly what to expect if he surrendered on the battlefield. An outsider such as Philip looking in on this hazing, or hearing garbled reports of it, might conclude that the Templars were initiating their members into a group based on the denial of Christ and the defamation of the cross. However, knowing the context of this event and its purpose as a lesson can perhaps change its understanding. If the ritual hazing truly occurred then I believe the Templars were not promoting heresies, but were merely reenacting Brother Roger's experience so that an initiate would think twice before surrendering to the Saracen and failing his habit, his brothers, and his God. Therefore the Templar initiation would have become not just a rite of passage for the future warrior monks but also a lesson to guide them in battle, in life, and in piety.

The many different accusations by Philip had to have originated somewhere. The issues and charges are complex, and reflect years of jealousy, secrecy, and intrigue towards the Templars. The "shock" which Philip and Clement both claim upon hearing the rumors of Templar heresy may not have been as genuine because heresies had existed in many institutions before and had been dealt with in the past. However, there must have been some credibility to the charges for Philip to believe that he could make a case to shut down an international order, and that he could convince the pope and kings throughout Christendom to go along. Philip's previous actions when he took down Boniface VIII and the Jewish banking institutions inside and outside his kingdom show what he was prepared to do in the name of "righteousness."

The Templars had been guilty at one time or another of major heresy, errors, and apostasies; they documented these failures within their *Rule*. Although the *Rule* itself was secret, and it was punishable to take it from chapter, copies could have been lost. A battle where a large number of Templars died could have made the looting of the *Rule* possible. It also could have been stolen, as the *Rule* itself states when describing an instance where the *Rule* was lost.

> And it happened that a German brother left the house at Chateau Pelerin and all his equipment was found except the *retrais*, which he kept. After a while the brother came to plead for mercy at the gate just as customary. The Master asked about it in chapter and there were brothers who said that they knew he had the *retrais*. And because they were not found, and he had not returned them, and it was not known what he had done with them, he was expelled from the house.[217]

If this is just one example of how the *Rule* could be lost, when the Templars were really struggling in the early fourteenth century, there is little that could keep someone like Philip from obtaining a copy whether by force, bribe, or theft. The Templars put all of their failures of

---

[217] Upton-Ward, *Catalan Rule,* 65-67.

house and habit within their *Rule*, so that new members would be read the *Rule* and hear of the horrors and punishments of individuals who failed their order and habit. Although meant as a tool to prevent such failures, which Barbara Frale suggests may even have been acted out; it seems possible that the *Rule* itself was a catalyst of their own undoing.

Bibliography

Aquinas, Thomas. *Summa Theologiae: A Concise Translation.* Edited by
    Timothy McDermott. Notre Dame: Christian Classics, 1991.

Barber, Malcolm. *The New Knighthood: A History of the Order of the
    Temple.* New York: Cambridge University Press, 2000.

_____, *The Trial of the Templars.* 2nd. New York: Cambridge
    University Press, 2006.

_____, and Keith Bate. *The Templars: Selected Sources Translated
    and Annotated.* New York: Manchester University Press, 2002.

Bernard of Clairvaux. "In Praise of the New Knighthood." In *Bernard of
    Clairvaux: Three Treatises.* Translated by Conrad Greenia, 127-
    145. Collegeville: Cistercian Publications, 1977.

Blum, Owen J, trans. *Peter Damian: Letters*, 6 vols. (the final two with
    Irven M. Resnick). The Fathers of the Church Mediaeval
    Continuation, 1-3 and 5-7 (Washington, DC: The Catholic
    University of America Press, 1989-2005).

Bradbury, Jim. *The Capetians.* New York: Continuum Books , 2007.

Bredero, Adriaan H. *Bernard of Clairvaux: Between Cult and History.*
    Grand Rapids: Eerdmans Publishing, 1996.

Brentano, Robert. *Two Churches: England and Italy in the Thirteenth
    Century.* Los Angeles: University of California Press, 1988.

Brown, Peter. *Augustine of Hippo.* Los Angeles: University of California
    Press, 2000.

Burgtorf, Jochen. *The Central Convent of Hospitallers and Templars:
    History, Organization, and Personnel (1099/1120-1310).*
    Boston: Brill, 2008.

Cantor, Norman F. *Inventing the Middle Ages.* New York: William
    Morrow and Company, 1991.

Constable, Giles. "The Ceremonies and Symbolism of Entering Religious Life and Taking the Monastic Habit from Fourth to the Twelfth Century." In *Segni e riti nella Chiesa altomedievale occidentale*. 2 vols. Settimane di studio del Centro italiano di studi sull'alto Medioevo, 33. Spoleto: CISAM, 1987. Vol. 2, pp. 771-834

_____, *The Reformation of the Twelfth Century*. New York: Cambridge University Press, 2002.

_____, *Three Treatises from Bec on the Nature of Monastic Life*. Translated by Bernard S. Smith. Toronto: Toronto University Press, 2008.

Curzon, Henri de. *La Régle du Temple*. Paris: La Société de l'histoire de France, 1886.

Dante. *The Divine Comedy*. Translated by Henry Wadsworth Longfellow. New York: Barnes & Noble, 2008.

Davis, Charles Wendell, trans. *The Conquest of Lisbon: De expugnatione Lyxbonensi*. New York: Columbia University Press, 2001.

Douglas, Mary. *Purity and Danger*. Harmondsworth: Penguin Books, 1970.

Duplessy, Jean. *Les Monnaies françaises royales*. Paris: Maison Platt, 1999.

Edbury, Peter W. *The Kingdom of Cyprus and the Crusades, 1191-1374*. New York: Cambridge University Press, 1991.

Eliade, Mircea. *The Sacred and the Profane: The Nature of Religion*. Translated by Willard R. Trask. New York: HBJ Publishers, 1987.

Favreau-Lilie, M. "The Military Orders and the Escape of the Christian Population from the Holy Land in 1291." *The Journal of Medieval History*, 19 (1993): 201-227.

Fawtier, Robert. *The Capetian Kings of France: Monarchy and Nation 987-1328.* New York: St. Martin's Press, 1978.

Forey, Alan. *The Fall of the Templars in the Crown of Aragon.* Burlington: Ashgate, 2001.

_____, *The Military Orders: From the Twelfth to the Early Fourteenth Centuries.* Toronto: University of Toronto Press, 1992.

Frale, Barbara. "The Chinon Chart: Papal Absolution to the Last Templar, Master Jacques de Molay." *Journal of Medieval History*, 30 (2004): 109-134.

_____, *The Templars.* Translated by Gregory Conti. New York: Arcade Publishing, 2009.

France, John. *Victory in the East.* New York: Cambridge University Press, 1994.

Gabrieli, Francesco. *Arab Historians of the Crusades.* Los Angeles: University of California Press, 1984.

Gennep, Arnold van. *The Rites of Passage.* Translated by Monika B. Vizedom and Gabrielle L. Caffee. Chicago: University of Chicago Press, 1960.

Gibbon, Edward. *The Decline and Fall of the Roman Empire.* New York: Macmillan Company, 1914.

Gilmour-Bryson, Anne. "Italian Templar Trials: Truth or Falsehood." In *Knighthoods of Christ: Essays on the History of the Crusades and the Knights Templar Presented to Malcolm Barber*, Edited by Norman Housley. Burlington: Ashgate, 2007.

_____, "Sodomy and the Knights Templar." *Journal of the History of Sexuality, no. 7* (1996): 151-183.

_____, trans. *The Trial of the Templars in Cyprus.* Boston: Brill, 1998.

85

_____, *The Trial of Templars in the Papal State and the Abruzzi*. Città del Vaticano: Biblioteca Apostolica Vaticana, 1982.

Ginzburg, Carlo. *The Cheese and the Worms: The Cosmos of a Sixteenth-Century Miller*. Baltimore: Johns Hopkins University Press, 1992.

Haag, Michael. *The Templars: The History & the Myth*. New York: Harper, 2009.

Hamilton, Bernard, "Rebuilding Zion: The Holy Places of Jerusalem in the Twelfth Century," in *Renaissance and Renewal in Christian History: Papers Read at the Fifteenth Summer Meeting and Sixteenth Winter Meeting of the Ecclesiastical History Society*. Edited by Derek Baker, Studies in Church History, 14. Oxford: Basil Blackwell, 1977.

Hopkins, Marilyn. *The Enigma of the Knights Templar: Their History and Mystical Connections* . St. Paul: Consortium Books, 2007.

Howe, John. *Church Reform & Social Change in Eleventh-Century Italy: Dominic of Sora and His Patrons*. Philadelphia: University of Pennsylvania Press, 1997.

InRebus.com. "The Chinon Parchment: Were the Knights Templar Pardoned ?" *In Rebus*. 2007. http://www.inrebus.com/chinon.php (accessed April 5, 2010).

Jerusalem Pilgrimage, 1099-1185. Edited by John Wilkinson, with Joyce Hill and W.F. Ryan. Hakluyt Society Works, 2nd ser., 167. London: Hakluyt Society, 1988.

Kardong, Terrence G. *Benedict's Rule: A Translation and Commentary*. Collegeville: The Liturgical Press, 1996.

Knighthoods of Christ: Essays on the History of the Crusades and the Knights Templar Presented to Malcolm Barber. Edited by Norman Housley. Burlington: Ashgate Publishing, 2007.

Ladner, Gerhart B. *The Idea of Reform: Its Impact on Christian Thought and Action in the Age of the Fathers.* Cambridge: Harvard University Press, 1959.

Lawrence, C.H. *Medieval Monasticism.* New York: Longman, 2001.

Lord, Evelyn. *The Knights Templar in Britain.* London: Longman, 2002.

Lynch, Joseph H. *The Medieval Church: A Brief History.* New York: Longman, 1992.

Madden, Thomas F. *The New Concise History of the Crusades (Student Edition).* Lanham: Rowman & Littlefield Publishers, 2006.

Menache, Sophia. *Clement V.* New York: Cambridge University Press, 1998.

Nicholson, Helen. *The Knights Templar: A New History.* Phoenix Mill: Sutton Publishing, 2001.

O'Callaghan, Joseph F. *Reconquest and Crusade in Medieval Spain.* Philadelphia: University of Pennsylvania Press, 2003.

Ogg, Frederic Austin. *A Source Book of Mediaeval History: Documents Illustrative of European Life and Institutions from the German Invasions to the Renaissance.* New York: Cooper Square Publishers, 1972.

Otto, Rudolf. *The Idea of the Holy.* New York: Oxford University Press, 1965.

Paine, Michael. *The Crusades.* Edison: Chartwell Books, 2005.

Phillips, Jonathan. *The Fourth Crusade and the Sack of Constantinople.* New York: Penguin Books, 2005.

Pringle, D. "Templar Castles on the Road to the Jordan." In *The Military Orders*: *Welfare and Warfare.* Edited by H. Nicholson, Aldershot: Ashgate Publishing, 1998. Pp.89-109.

Read, Piers Paul. *The Templars.* New York: St. Martin's Griffin, 2009.

Reynolds, Barbara. *Dante: The Poet, the Political Thinker, the Man.* United Kingdom: Shoemaker Hoard, 2006.

Riley-Smith, Jonathan. *The Crusades: A Short History.* New Haven: Yale University Press, 1987.

_____, *The Feudal Nobility and the Kingdom of Jerusalem 1174-1277.* London: Archon Books, 1973.

_____, *The Oxford Illustrated History of the Crusades.* New York: · Oxford University Press, 1995.

_____. "The Structures of the Orders of the Temple and the Hospital." In *The Medieval Crusade.* Edited.by Susan J. Ridyard. Woodbridge: Boydell Press, 2004. Pp.125-143.

Roulx, J. Delaville le. *Un nouveau manuscrit de la Régle du Temple (Biliolife Reprint).* Lexington, Kentucky: BiblioLife, 2010.

Runciman, Steven. *The First Crusade (Canto Edition).* Cambridge: Cambridge University Press, 1992.

Saewulf. "The Travels of Saewulf." In *The Crusades: A Reader.* Edited by S. J. Allen and Emilie Amt. Peterborough: Broadview Press, 2003. Pp. 99-103.

Schein, Sylvia. *Fideles Crucis: the Papacy, the West, and the Recovery of the Holy Land, 1274-1314.* New York: Oxford University Press, 1991.

_____."Philip IV the Fair and the Crusade: A Reconsideration." In *Crusade and Settlement: Papers Read at the First Conference of the Society for the Study of the Crusades and the Latin East and Presented to R.C. Smail.* Edited by Peter W. Edbury. Atlantic Highlands: Humanities Press, 1985.

Schnürer, Gustav. *Die Ursprüngliche Templeregel: Vergleich der lateinischen und der französischen Ausgabe der Regel.* Freiburg im Breisgau: Herder, 1903.

Strayer, Joseph. *The Reign of Philip the Fair*. Princeton: Princeton University Press, 1980.

"The Latin Rule of 1129." In *The Templars: Selected Sources Translated and Annotated*, edited by Malcolm Barber and Keith Bate. Manchester: Manchester University Press, 2002. Pp.31-54.

Upton-Ward, Judi, trans. *The Catalan Rule of the Templars*. Woodbridge: The Boydell Press, 2003.

Upton-Ward, Judi, trans. *The Rule of the Templars: The French Text of the Rule of the Order of the Knights Templar*. Rochester, NY: Boydell and Brewer, 2008.

White, Lynn. *Medieval Technology and Social Change*. Oxford: Oxford University Press, 1964.

William of Tyre. *A History of Deeds Done beyond the Sea, by William, Archbishop of Tyre*. Translated by Emily Atwater Babcock and A.C. Krey. New York: Columbia University Press, 1943.

_____. *Historia rerum in partibus transmarinis gestarum*. Translated by James Brundage. In *The Crusades: A Documentary History*. Milwaukee: Marquette University Press, 1962.

Winter, Michael, Amalia Levanoni, eds. *The Mamluks in Egyptian and Syrian Politics and Society*. Leiden: Brill, 2004.

Wolfe, Eric R. *Europe and the People Without History*. Los Angeles: University of California Press, 1990.

Wood, Charles. *Philip the Fair and Boniface VIII*. New York: Holt, Rinehart and Winston, 1967.

21040551R00056

Printed in Great Britain
by Amazon